# Brand Design Secrets

## Design a Magnetic Brand and Company Image in Just 1 Day

### (With Very Little Money, Without Any Design Skills)

**Curtis Floth**

UntappedCustomers.com

**Brand Design Secrets: Design a Magnetic Brand and Company Image In Just 1 Day (With Very Little Money, Without Any Design Skills)**

All Rights Reserved.

First Printing: July 2021
Curtis Floth
Copyright © 2021 Curtis Floth
ISBN: 978-1-7374521-0-2

# Why Read This Book

———— ❧ ————

Are you tired of your business not getting the exposure and customers it needs? You have a logo and a superior product, but you lose customers to the competition. You buy ads and get people to your website, but few people buy. You want to earn a living helping people, but everyone wants you to lower your prices.

The truth is that most businesses are not as successful as they could be because they have not designed a brand that attracts their best customers. Customers are willing to pay a higher price for a brand that's perfect for them.

Are you ready to attract better customers, and more of them?

In this book, I will share the step-by-step system I use to quickly create a brand strategy and design for very little money, even if you don't have any design skills. It's the perfect system for uncovering how to stand out in a crowded market and attract your ideal customers.

# Written by a Startup Designer with 25 Years of Experience

———— ❧ ————

Curtis Floth is a startup designer with over 25 years of experience. He helps new businesses understand their audience, launch their brands, and grow their businesses online. Entrepreneurs come to him when they need a website that attracts and converts their best buyers, which he achieves through a potent blend of marketing, programming, and design. You could say he's a certified web geek with the unique ability to look at your online business from every single angle.

But here's the problem - before you can even get started on designing a money-making website or funnel, you first need to get clear on your brand identity. Understandably, this is where new business owners get stuck.

Through decades of working with many startups and small businesses, Curtis discovered a way to turn his hard-wired intuition into a step-by-step process for small business owners to follow.

# Table of Contents

# Brand Design & Clarity

—————— ❧ ——————

Have you ever owned a pair of Crocs? Ever personalized your Crocs by adding some Jibbitz?

Rich and Sheri Schmelzer held a check in their hands for ten million dollars. This payout was the direct result of paying attention to branding and marketing. Just over a year before, they were at their kitchen table helping their kids decorate their Crocs shoes with ribbons and buttons.

From the simple idea of personalizing Crocs, they started the Jibbitz company. That's when it all turned around for them. Soon the company was multiplying month after month. Over a year later they sold the company to Crocs shoes for ten million dollars and even made an appearance on the Oprah Winfrey show.

Without attention to branding and marketing, Rich and Sheri's story would not have turned out so great.

Today you've probably checked your sales for yesterday and discovered only a few new sales, if any at all.

Are you tired of your business not getting the exposure it deserves and not attracting more customers? The problem is not your product or service.

The problem is you're not getting enough exposure to customers and exciting them about your brand. The tricky part is that it's not always evident to you when your branding is wrong.

You have a great logo and a superior product, but you still lose customers to the competition.

You buy ads and get people to your website, but only a very few people buy.

You want to earn a living helping people and providing a service, but everyone wants you to lower your prices.

The truth is that most businesses are not as successful as they could be because they have not designed a brand that attracts their best customers.

The reasons for Apple's success go beyond

Steve Job's leadership. Apple became what it is today because Steve Jobs understood branding and marketing too.

In 1984 Apple launched the first Macintosh under the leadership of Steve Jobs. Reviews of the Macintosh were great, but sales were terrible. The following year, Apple's Board of Directors forced him out of the company he started.

The remaining leadership kept Apple going, but by 1997 it was in bad shape. The company reported its worst quarter ever and was nearly bankrupt. That's when Steve Jobs started turning the company around.

One month after leading the company again, Steve Jobs introduced the "Think Different" campaign—a marketing campaign that didn't try to appeal to everyone. Instead, it was a marketing campaign that was a rallying cry to their perfect customers.

That's when Apple stopped competing on features and functionality.

That's when Apple started becoming the brand it is today.

That's when Steve Jobs brought his understanding of branding and marketing back to Apple.

You can have a brand just as powerful as Apple, but you must start paying attention to your branding and marketing. And your customers will be willing to pay you a higher price because the quality of your company will improve.

The good news is you don't have to spend a fortune to design your brand. You don't have to spend months on focus groups and market research. You only have to get started.

Did you know that Nike only paid $35 for their first logo? Since then, they have changed their logo four times. Apple has changed its logo seven times and Starbucks five times.

As your company grows to six, seven, eight figures and beyond, your brand is going to change. Today all you need to do is design a winning brand for your company as it is right now.

What's not going to change is that people want to be associated with a positive brand. Customers are naturally attracted to brands they know, like, and trust.

In this book, I will share the step-by-step system I use to quickly create a brand strategy and design for very little money, even if you don't have any design skills.

It's the same system I use to help companies swiftly establish a brand strategy and design for their brand. It's the perfect system for uncovering how to stand out in a crowded market and attract your ideal customers.

But I haven't always had this system or paid enough attention to branding.

I've been a startup designer for over twenty-five years, helping companies just starting to grow their online presence—whether it's creating their web apps or apps, designing their marketing sites, building their social media presence, and much more.

The companies would often already have a logo but not a plan for branding the rest of the business. I loved these situations early on in my career for different reasons than today. Back then, I saw these as chances to express creative freedom, sprinkle in the latest design trends, and build my design portfolio.

Then the dot-com bubble burst and the startup I

was working for ran out of funding. I was handed my pink slip and sent to the unemployment line. In a flash, I went from getting daily requests from recruiters to being one of thirty or more applying for a single job.

I spent the next three years hopping from job to job, trying to find solid ground. I would start working for a company only to get laid off soon after. Eventually, the job opportunities stopped coming in and I spent two years living off unemployment and credit cards—completely unsure of what I was going to do and scared out of my mind.

Then one day, I got a call from my friends at Jibbitz. The company was growing at an incredible rate, and they were having a hard time keeping up. I joined the team to help with their e-commerce and marketing. I was eventually overseeing their trade shows and consumer order fulfillment.

Working with Jibbitz was the first time I got to design and implement a brand strategy beyond a website. We had to create delightful experiences at every touchpoint with the company. From store displays to trade show booths, product designs, packaging, and, of course, the e-commerce website.

We created ways to have a better understanding of what the stores needed and what customers wanted. Then we took action on those insights. The changes resulted in delighted customers who loved the company and the brand.

After the Jibbitz experience, I continued learning more about branding and marketing. I then used my knowledge and expertise to help companies find opportunities to stand out and get noticed.

Today, I am still assisting companies in getting attention as well as delight from their customers.

Large corporations can spend years and millions of dollars on rebranding. With in-depth market research, strategy sessions, creativity workshops, and testing, they can create their perfect next brand. Unfortunately, startups don't have the time or budget for focus groups and week-long strategy workshops. They need to design their brand fast and focus on growing the business.

For the past twelve years, I have learned everything I can about human behavior, marketing, and branding. I had to start finding processes and online tools to simplify the brand strategy process, distilling it down into exercises a company can accomplish in hours, not weeks.

I get frustrated when I see companies paying five figures for brand design when they're not even making five figures a month yet. When a business is making less than five figures a month, changes and pivots can happen frequently. The company needs to be able to adjust its brand quickly when those changes occur. And paying thousands in rebranding costs with every pivot isn't cost-effective.

The formula that I'm going to share applies to any size of business. It's perfect for new projects, startups, and small businesses that need a customer-attracting brand. I promise that after reading the pages in this book and implementing the process, your business is going to get more attention, more customers, and more five-star reviews. More importantly, you will be able to stop competing on price and grow your business.

As you turn the next page and start reading the next chapter, remember, these exercises shouldn't take months or thousands of dollars to complete. Instead, you can go through the entire system quickly. You can even complete the whole journey in as little as one day. How fast you go through the process is up to you.

Along the way, you'll design your brand. You'll also gain clarity about the company's image behind the brand design—paving the way for more effective marketing and naturally attracting more of your perfect customers.

# Forces Working Against You

————— ❧ —————

Some forces don't want you to be successful at branding and marketing. Many times, though, it's yourself that is standing in your way;

- "I don't have time for branding."
- "Branding is cute and all, but I need to get customers."
- "I have a logo, and that's good enough."
- "I don't want to pay for a design that I'm not going to like."
- "I don't need a brand. I just need the right funnel and ads."

When you get clear on what you want your brand to be, the marketing is easier and more effective.

There are also forces you can't control:

- Everyone is busy.
- Everyone constantly gets bombarded with ads.
- Everyone has the attention of a goldfish.

There is a difference between trust and attention. Attention gets people to notice your ad, but it takes trust to get them to buy from you—especially the first time.

People have to see a logo three to five times before they recognize it. But they need far more contacts with your company before they buy—sometimes as many as twenty or thirty touchpoints. Retargeting ads work as well as they do because they incorporate multiple touches. They are building trust and reminding prospects that they are missing out on an opportunity.

Don't get me wrong. It is possible to get people to buy something the first time they see an ad. But it's challenging. The advantages of purchasing the offer must far exceed the disadvantages of them possibly wasting money, looking foolish, and losing valuable time.

Then after someone buys from you, they continue experiencing your company. This time, they're getting the exclusive inside experience. (That's not something everyone gets to see.) And every step along their journey, they're forming an opinion about your business. Ultimately, that opinion will determine what reviews they leave for you and what they tell others about you.

"Your brand is what other people say about you when you're not in the room."

Jeff Bezos, Founder of Amazon

Designing your brand helps define how you want that experience to feel for your customers and your team. Once you've determined the experience, you can ensure every touchpoint is in alignment.

Imagine these as four wheels on a car:

- Logo
- Culture
- Marketing
- Customer experience

Designing your brand ensures all four wheels are going in the same direction. When everything is in alignment, your business can move forward faster and grow.

If one wheel is not in alignment, customers get mixed messages about your company. Your business looks amateur and unprofessional. More customers become confused about your business, and fewer buy.

Every company already has a brand, from your local dry cleaners or Chinese food restaurant to the person who cuts your hair. People talk about your business, and it has a reputation. Or, even worse, no one talks about your business. Designing your brand turns it into the type of business your ideal customers want to work with.

A friend recently sold his Infiniti SUV because he didn't need a seven-passenger vehicle anymore. He wanted to buy a luxury car but wasn't sure which one to buy. He used to own a Mercedes E550 and loved it. But these days, Mercedes doesn't make the E550 or the S550.

He went to a Mercedes dealership to test-drive the latest Mercedes models and left the dealership depressed. He didn't love the new models the way he did his old E550. So he had to look at other luxury car brands.

Back home, he started researching cars to test-drive next. Eventually, he found the Maserati Ghibli and decided to give it a try. After sitting in the car, he immediately recognized the window control buttons on the door. His friend's Dodge had the same buttons, which seemed odd because Maserati is an Italian brand.

But many of the luxury vehicle brands are owned by large conglomerate auto groups. Maserati is part of Chrysler Fiat. Audi owns Lamborghini. Volkswagen owns Bugatti and Porsche. And it's common for these large auto groups to share auto parts among brands to help reduce costs and improve profits.

Buttons and controls are part of the experience. You see and touch them every time you go somewhere. Sharing these parts may help reduce costs but are at the sacrifice of the brand experience.

Imagine you spent $120,000 on a Maserati. Then, later on, find yourself in a Dodge or Jeep and discover the same buttons and controls all around you.

How would that change the driving experience in your $120,000 Maserati?

How would that affect your decision the next time you're in the market for a new car?

What seems like a small change can have a significant impact on the reputation of a brand. Too many business owners choose to design the brand image how they want it—ignoring what the market is looking for or needs. But when people are selecting a product or service, they always pick what's best for them—not what's best for your business.

Choosing to ignore the market means that your company could be missing out on building a solid customer base and connecting with people. Or worse, your brand could end up getting ignored by customers and fail to grow.

You can design a brand that attracts the perfect customers and builds brand loyalty. The Magnetic Brand Method gives you everything you need to create a winning brand. I break the process into three sections: market opportunities, logo design, and brand kit design. Each section has a system of steps designed to help you uncover the perfect brand and create it.

This gives you three *huge* payoffs:

1. You get to harness the millions of dollars other companies have spent on branding and research.

2. You clarify your brand image to let prospects know you're right for them.

3. You develop a memorable and clear presence

that cuts through the noise and gets noticed.

It sounds simple enough, but the journey is no longer than three steps. The Magnetic Brand Method helps guide you along every step of the way.

I'll go into immense detail about the Magnetic Brand Method in the methodology section later. But, briefly, the process uses a unique system for gathering data about your business and market. You'll then take action on that information in a precise way to design your perfect brand;

a brand with a personality and presence that you enjoy and attracts customers you like working with—a brand that you are proud of and happy to have created.

The roots of the Magnetic Brand Method are in traditional brand strategy, but the approach is different. The startups and small businesses I've worked with needed strong branding. But they were limited on time and budget.

As Paul Buchheit of Y Combinator advises, I looked for the "90/10 solution" for every step in a traditional brand strategy process. I needed to find a way to accomplish 90% of designing a brand with only 10% of the effort and time. The result is a brand design process that jump-starts your company's brand strategy and gets you moving.

You can complete the Magnetic Brand Method in as little as three hours. The longest part of the process is designing your logo. If you decide to design the logo yourself, the amount of time you spend creating it is entirely up to you. Working with a designer or agency can take three to five days or more, depending on the designer.

The best part of the Magnetic Brand Method is how much time (and money) you'll save. Your website and funnels must look professional to build trust. Good branding agencies are great to work with, but spending thousands of dollars on branding upfront is a challenging way to start.

Instead, follow the Magnetic Brand Method and get your brand started now. Later you can invest in hiring a branding agency—after the company has grown large enough and you're ready to take it to the next level. This approach reduces your up-front risk. It also gives you the flexibility to adjust your brand if your company needs to pivot.

If you decide to hire a logo designer, you can save even more time. You can let them craft the perfect logo for your brand while you work on the rest of the business. Hiring a logo designer might seem too risky right now. But in this book, I will show you how to find the right designer for your brand—giving you more confidence that your logo will become what you want it to be.

The big secret that makes this method even more effective comes from human behavior, specifically the law of attraction. It's the key ingredient that your competition is likely ignoring.

When you position your brand in a certain way, it naturally becomes more attractive to your customers. It feels more comfortable and recognizable to them, helping you build trust with your perfect customers faster. I will show you exactly how to take advantage of this human trait as part of designing your logo.

I created the Magnetic Brand Method to help companies earning $10,000 or less per month. But it can also help companies making more than that by guiding them to where there are more opportunities for their brand.

Not all branding agencies are the same. If your company is earning more than $10,000 a month, the exercises in this book will help you figure out where you need to take your brand to in its next phase. You can then use that information to hire the perfect branding agency that will get you there.

But when your company is earning less than $10,000 per month, keeping costs low is essential. It's even more critical for companies that are just getting started. Since I don't know where your business is today, I will show you several options to fit your budget. I will show you how to create your logo on your own for free, how to hire a logo designer for less than $300, and many more options available to you.

Wherever your company is today, it's reasonable to invest in branding and rebranding as your company grows and changes. As you'll see, even the largest brands in the world go through a rebranding from time to time. Set a budget and follow the Magnetic Brand Method for your brand. Then you can set a larger budget and rebrand your company whenever you feel it's the right move. How often you update your brand's image is up to you—this book gives you the tools to speed up the process.

You don't need design skills to complete the process. But you will need to have opinions on what you want and don't want for your brand. I will show you how to find a designer that can create something you'll love within your budget, even if you have zero design skills. You must, however, be willing to listen to the market. Success relies on creating a brand you're proud of and one the market enjoys.

Branding directly impacts the success of your business. It's challenging to get new customers and keep the ones you have when your business mainly gets ignored. Make the time to go through the process and turn your business into a brand.

The clarity you will find will make all your marketing efforts more straightforward and faster— from the products and services you provide to the social media posts and ads. They all thrive when built on a solid brand foundation.

After your business steps into its brand, the market knows your company, who you best serve, and why your offerings are valuable. Your business attracts customers that are perfect for you. They love your company's attention and feel valued. They don't hesitate to tell others about you when they know you can help.

Imagine your business having a brand and reputation that people know and love. Imagine having less worry and stress about where your next customers will come from. Imagine the heavy weight of anxiety about paying bills and being successful lifted from your shoulders. Prospects will know that you genuinely improve the lives of others while also improving your life and your family's lives. Owning a business isn't easy; imagine how it will feel when others see what you accomplished with your company.

And it all starts with your company's brand. Your brand is not just a logo but the company behind the logo too. You can run a logo contest or buy a random symbol to mark the task complete. But if you ignore the branding part, the market will fail to see meaning in that logo. It won't connect with the hearts of your perfect customers. It won't stand out and get you the exposure you deserve.

It doesn't matter if your company is brand new or

has been around for years. Now is the time to build the meaning behind your company logo. Now is the time to help your customers change their lives and scale your business. Now is the time to design the perfect brand for your company and stand out.

Your customers are out there waiting for you. They desperately need your help and are willing to pay you for it. But they don't hear your message through all the noise. Are you ready to cut through the noise and change their lives? If so, your brand is the first step, and I'm with you every step of the way.

# What to Do When Your
# Logo Sucks

——— ❧ ———

One of the most common questions I get from business owners is, "I already have a logo. Will this method help my business?" The simple answer is "Yes." Many people think that branding is just designing the logo and picking some colors, but it's so much more. Your company logo is a symbol representing your business. Your brand is the emotional connection and reputation with people. If you already have a logo, the Magnetic Brand Method will help you build a brand with that logo. Of course, that all depends on the quality of your current logo.

The reality is your logo has to be REALLY bad for people to say something; really, really bad. If you ask friends what they think about your logo, they will typically hold back their opinions. They'll tell you that it's okay or that it looks good with maybe a suggestion here or there.

Meanwhile, the market is a harsher critic. But even the market won't tell you that your logo is terrible. They aren't worried about hurting your feelings—they don't know you. But they aren't going to go out of their way to give you their opinion either. Instead, they're worried about overcoming their own challenges, maintaining their status quo, and saving their hard-earned money.

When your logo is terrible, it's easily forgotten, and prospects won't remember you when they need you. When your logo looks amateurish, people expect low prices, and you lose more business to the competition. The result of a bad logo and branding is not harsh criticism but missed opportunities and lower revenue.

A good logo is simple and represents the best of the company. The Nike swoosh is just a shape showing movement. Branding and marketing have shown you the stories and emotions that the logo represents. Branding and marketing turned that simple shape into something that has meanings and emotions behind it.

My friend Rosemary was an ER doctor and ready for a career change. In late 2020, she decided to switch to real estate and help people find homes they loved. She could leverage her network of doctors and medical professionals to find clients. But she was faced with a real challenge when deciding on her brand and company name.

She looked at the names of the more prominent real estate companies for inspiration. Most of the local companies used their last name. But her last name was difficult to spell and remember. She brainstormed names using rose and rosebud, playing off her first name. But none of them seemed right. She turned to her Facebook friends for help:

"Okay guys, I need your help and suggestions. Trying to come up with a name for my realty business that's easier to say and remember than my last name, but that might help people at least remember part of my name. Like 'Rosemary G from x realty.'"

I contacted Rosemary and told her about my Magnetic Brand Method. I explained how it could help her design a brand for her real estate business and find a great name. We set up an afternoon to get her started. By that evening, she had completed the market opportunities tasks.

Through the process, she realized that she wanted to help busy professionals the most. Professionals that weren't afraid to accomplish goals and be successful. She wanted to be their trusted advisor while assisting them in finding the right home for their discerning taste.

Soon after, we came up with a great name and started following the steps of the Magnetic Brand Method. She was able to find the right logo designer quickly. She and her designer went through a few logo iterations before landing on the perfect logo and brand. With her new brand complete, she started her business.

Using the same steps in this book, Rosemary went from a business without a name to an attractive brand in a very short time. Plus, she was armed with the precise direction of her new business, knowing who her perfect customers were and how to attract them. A few weeks later, she had her first listing on the market.

By following the Magnetic Brand Method, you will clarify the brand and business you want your logo to represent—the meanings and emotions that will stand out from your competition and attract your perfect customers, turning your current logo into a brand. Along the way, you get to decide if your current logo is the best representation of your company or not.

You may find that your current logo works for your business. Great! You will build a brand around your existing logo. You will uncover ways to use branding to help the logo stand out in the market, filling in the missing pieces needed to complete your brand image and emotionally connect with prospects. You may also find that your business has outgrown your current symbol, and it's time to replace it.

The idea of replacing a logo you spent time and money on designing might not seem like an option. And I'm not saying you will have to change it for sure. But I recommend keeping an open and objective mind about your logo. After all, it's not just your opinion of it that matters. It's the opinion of your market as well, especially those of your target customers.

Every company should be willing to change its logo at some point. It doesn't mean the company wasted money on their old one. After all, the old logo got them to where they are. It means the company knows more now than it did before. It also means the company is going after new opportunities to grow and connect.

I have designed many logos that I loved, but the market didn't like. I've worked with startups that have failed to capture attention and ultimately floundered. I've also worked with several startups that made the proper connections with the market and multiplied. One of the most important lessons is that you can't just guess what will work. You must be willing to gather data and make informed decisions.

Designing a brand and logo is like trying to pick winning lottery numbers. You could choose different numbers every time you play. You could pick the same numbers every time. You could even let the computer pick numbers for you. But none of these approaches increase your odds of winning.

But what if you had a way to find out the first two numbers before the drawing? Gathering that little bit of information would help you make an informed decision on all the numbers to pick and dramatically increase your odds of winning something.

Data-driven decisions are at the heart of the Magnetic Brand Method. You will gather little bits of information quickly to help you make informed brand decisions. I encourage you to go through the entire method. And if you don't want to change the logo, that's okay. You can simply skip the part about designing your logo and continue.

If you're not sure if your logo is good or not, that's okay. In the Market Opportunity section, I'll give you a simple way to find out if your logo is truly good or not. I will show you how to turn that good logo into a great brand.

You'll be excited about updating your website, social media profiles, and marketing materials. You'll have a better sense of direction of where you want to take the company and be ready to show the market your company's new image and value. Creating a brand for your business is an exciting and rewarding experience.

Today, there's no denying the importance of having a solid brand strategy. Branding can make all the difference when you're trying to attract new customers. If you don't have a strong brand, it can be tough to stand out and be memorable.

You can design a brand that attracts the perfect customers and builds brand loyalty. It all starts with the first step. Before you know it, your brand will get the exposure and attention it deserves.

# Magnetic Brand Method Part I
# Market Opportunities

———— ❧ ————

## Step 1
## Your Target Audiences

**Before Getting Started**

There are a few simple tasks you need to do to prepare for the journey ahead.

First, you will be creating several Pinterest boards along the way. So you'll need to create a free Pinterest account if you don't already have one.

Visit Pinterest.com and sign up for a free account. After you sign up, they will ask you to follow a few steps to set up your account. Follow the steps and come back to this book. Don't worry about creating a board yet. I'll show you how to do that part later.

Next, you will need to get your copy of the Magnetic Brand Worksheet. It's a Google Doc that

I created for you. To access it, visit the following web address:

branddesignsecrets.com/resources

The worksheet is your starting point for everything you will be doing in Part 1 of the Magnetic Brand Method. Download or make a copy of the worksheet.

When you have a copy of the worksheet, make sure you can make changes to it. You're now ready to move on to the next step!

**Define Your Target Audiences**

The first step in building any marketing campaign is defining your target audience. Designing your brand is no different. So why do I want you to pick target audiences? The answer is messaging and branding that connects.

There's a common misconception among small business owners that their business needs to cater to everyone. If they don't use branding that appeals to everyone, their business will suffer. It's simply not true. Instead, the opposite is true.

Even the largest corporations don't cater to everyone. Amazon knows you are not a target customer for their online store if you don't shop online. If you want a personal assistant or concierge to help you with your shopping, Walmart knows their stores are not for you.

Those giant corporations need to make massive amounts of money every month so they can pay their bills and keep their shareholders happy. That means they need to appeal to more people and more audiences. It also means that their branding and messaging need to be broader and more general.

As a small business, you have an advantage those large corporations don't have. You can appeal to the hearts of target audiences better than they can. For example, you can create a brand experience that lets them know you understand them and what they're going through. And that you're there to help them through it.

After all, you only need one hundred people paying you one hundred dollars a month to have a five-figure a month business. You don't need millions of followers yet. You need millions of likes. You only need a core group of people that know, like, and trust you. And then they will happily tell others about you every chance they get.

If all this hasn't convinced you to focus on your target audiences, then think about the worst customer you have ever had. Remember what it was like to work with that customer. Then think about how you felt when you finally finished working with them.

Do you want more customers like them in your business?

Probably not. Which means you don't want everyone as a customer for your business. You only want some of the people. So what are some customer traits you want to avoid in the future?

Why not make it easier and focus on those customers that are perfect for your products or services? The ones that genuinely need your help.

Focusing on target audiences makes your marketing and branding easier. That's because everyone is different—with different challenges, experiences, and perspectives.

Features can mean different things to different audiences.

Let's take the feature of a four-wheel drive, for example. To a specific audience, a four-wheel drive means that you can keep adventuring on the trail when your friends have to turn back in their vehicles. But to others, a four-wheel drive means being able to get the kids to their activity, even in the worst of weather. So it's the same feature but has different benefits to different audiences.

When you focus your company on your target audiences, you talk about the benefits that matter to them instead of just the features. When combined with a relatable brand, your audience feels like they belong.

I like to use an archery target when thinking about audiences for a brand. Your primary audience is the bullseye at the center. They are the people you're directly speaking to. They are the ones you focus your marketing and messaging.

Your secondary audiences are the ring just outside the bullseye. You're not speaking directly to them. But they might hear the message, and it may resonate with them.

Then you have your other audiences in the second ring outside the bullseye. They might hear you speaking to your primary audience. But it doesn't resonate with them as well as those in your primary or secondary audiences.

The secondary and other audiences are optional. Keeping those audiences empty is okay.

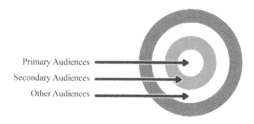

Primary Audiences
Secondary Audiences
Other Audiences

For example, let's say you had a company that helps soccer moms. They're your primary audience. So you're messaging around a mom with kids that are into soccer.

Your secondary audience might be soccer dads.

The soccer dads will probably hear the messaging as well. You may not be directly talking to them, but they might listen to the message and still understand it and be interested in it.

Kids soccer coaches might be another one of your other audiences. They might hear the messaging from the moms or dads or come across it themselves. They may not be interested in what you're offering but are around those that are.

Who are your primary audience, your secondary, and your other audiences? Again, you can leave the secondary and other audiences empty.

In your worksheet, start to list your primary, secondary, and other audiences.

You can have up to four primary audiences. You can have up to five secondary audiences. And up to ten for your other audiences. Each list has a limit to help focus your company and brand because when your company is smaller, you want everything focused on those specific audiences. When your company gets to making $10,000 or more per month, you can start adding more audiences. But even then, your marketing will tend to focus on specific groups of people.

If you aren't sure of your audiences, think about each one of your products and services. Try to figure out your primary audiences for it. When explaining the benefits of its features, who do those benefits appeal to?

The secondary and other audiences are optional. You can leave them blank if you want. But add at least one group to your primary audiences list.

**Your Primary Customer Avatars**

After you have your target audience, let's focus on your primary audiences. You should have at least one audience group on your list and no more than four.

For each audience on your primary audience list, think of a person that best represents the audience. Ideally, it's someone you've met before, but they don't have to be a real person. Instead, you can take the traits of many people you know and create the person to represent the audience.

Let's say one of your target audiences is soccer moms, for example. Think of a person you've met that best represents what a soccer mom is to you. What does her average day look like? What are some challenges that she struggles with? What qualities does she have that let you know that she is a soccer mom?

Now, look at the first group on your primary audience list. Think of a person you've met that best represents that audience to you. Only you and people helping you with marketing will ever see this information. So don't avoid using someone because it might make a wrong impression on someone else.

What goals do they want to accomplish? What challenges are frustrating them? What are some qualities or traits that you know are part of that audience? Once you have that person in mind, give them a first name. It could be their real first name, or you can make up a name.

In your worksheet, move to the Primary Customer Names section. Then add in the table below the name of your primary audience and the representative person's first name. That is to say, the first name of the person you just thought of that best represents that primary audience.

Next, let's turn those representative people into your brand's customer avatars. Move to the Primary Customer Avatars section of the worksheet. Fill out the customer avatar information for each of the people that represent your primary audiences. You can put as little or as much information as you like. Start by adding their first name.

In the Description section, put information that will remind your future self who this person is and what they mean to your business.

Under Demographics, list the person's characteristics such as age, gender, income, and education.

The Hobbies/Interests section is where you can list activities and hobbies the person enjoys. They may be related to your business or not, but they help give a better understanding of who this person is.

For Goals, put in information you believe the person wants to accomplish that relates to your business. They can be goals you directly help them achieve. Or goals that help you identify them as part of that audience.

The Frustrations section is for writing down the barriers that are blocking them from accomplishing their goals.

Finally, in the Brands They Like section, list any brands you can think of that they like, follow, or buy—especially brands that let you know they are part of that audience.

Start filling in your Primary Customer Avatars. This step can seem like it could take a long time to finish but you can set a time limit. I like to give 20–30 minutes to complete this step. You don't need every detail about the customer avatar right now. You can add information any time you think of new things. For now, just write down enough information to remind you of who that person is.

From now on, stop thinking about the audience and start thinking about the people you just picked. Each individual represents a larger audience. Thinking this way will make it easier for you to design a brand that attracts your primary audiences.

But it's helpful to put a face with a name. So add a picture of the person for each of your customer avatars. Grab an image from their social media profiles if they're real people or from stock photography. You could even pick a photo from generator.photos to use.

After you have added a photo to each customer avatar, they are complete for now. These avatars represent your primary audiences. Over time, you might learn more information about each avatar. You can update your avatars at any time, and I encourage you to keep them up to date. They will help you with your marketing well after you have finished designing your brand.

# Step 2
# Your Competition

— ❖ —

Many business owners think of competition as being all bad. But there are benefits to having competition. Competition drives improvement and forces you to get out of your comfort zone. It encourages you to specialize rather than focus on an extensive skill set.

There's also an opportunity for you to learn from their marketing efforts. They're spending marketing dollars promoting their business. So attention to what they're doing and see what's working for them. Then learn from what you see them doing.why not pay

From my perspective, there are three different types of business competition:

- Direct competition
- Indirect competition
- Alternatives

**Direct competition** is when another company is selling **similar products or services** to the same audience. For example, if I had a company selling coffee mugs to coffee drinkers, a company that is also selling coffee mugs to coffee drinkers is my direct competition.

**Indirect competition** is when another company sells **different products or services** to the same audience. Again, let's say I'm selling coffee mugs to coffee drinkers. A company that is selling coffee beans to coffee drinkers is my indirect competition.

**Alternatives** are actions the customer can take instead of buying any product or service from my company or my competition.

Here's another way to think about competition. When your customer avatar is looking for the product or service you offer:

- Will they buy EITHER yours or the other company's product or service?
- Or will they buy BOTH?

If they usually buy both, then the other company is an indirect competitor.

In your worksheet, go to the Your Brand's

Competition section. Then start adding your brand's competition to the three lists: Direct competition, Indirect competition, and Alternatives. Up to five direct companies or brands. Up to ten indirect companies or brands. And up to ten alternatives.

Don't go past those limits because it will start to get overwhelming. If a list gets too long, pick the companies, brands, and alternatives you often compete with—the companies or brands that you want to stand out from the most.

**Create a Direct Competition Pinterest Board**

Pinterest is an excellent tool for collecting inspiration for room decor and dinner ideas. It's also a great tool to help design a brand that stands out. Log in (or sign up) to Pinterest.com and create a new board named "Brand Competition." You can choose to "Keep this board secret" if you want.

Pin images to the board that represent the brands of your competition. You can add whatever photos and graphics remind you of their brand. At a minimum, include the logo of each of your competitors. I like to add screenshots of their website home page and landing pages. I may also add pictures of their marketing materials, such as display ads or brochures.

Start with pinning images of your direct competition. After you've added all of them, you can add your indirect competitors if you want. You will be using this Pinterest board to reference brands your company needs to stand out from. Have enough brands on the board that you can find ways to stand out but not so many that it becomes overwhelming. Three to five different brands is usually enough.

After you have added all the pins to your Pinterest board, scroll through the images. Do you notice any patterns? Do the brands look very similar or very different? It's usually surprising what information gets uncovered through this exercise.

**Your Competitive Advantages**

In business, having a competitive advantage is crucial. It means you have the edge over your competitors and can take your business to the next level. But what exactly is it? A competitive advantage is something that makes your business stand apart from all others. Something that makes your company the clear choice for your target audience. If you can identify your competitive advantage, you can use it to find untapped customers.

I've learned there are two types of competitive advantages to think about: unique benefits and unique methods.

Unique benefits are benefits to your product or service that your competitors don't have. Nicotine gum, for example, helps to clean teeth and helps people quit smoking. Helping to clean teeth is a benefit that nicotine patches can't provide. This makes "helps clean teeth" a unique benefit to nicotine gum.

Unique methods are the specific processes, systems, or recipes only found in your company or brand. The formula for Coca-Cola is an excellent example of a unique method. Only Coca-Cola has that specific flavor. Pepsi and other cola beverage makers have tastes similar to Coca-Cola, but they are not the same. The only way to get that exact flavor is to buy from Coca-Cola.

As a small business owner, it's easy to feel pressure to lower prices or offer a better selection just to compete. But there's another way: create a unique method that helps you stand out from the crowd and win clients over. Then you are no longer competing on price alone because the process is only available from your brand.

You may not think you have a secret recipe, but you do. Most unique methods are in the journey customers make while working with your brand. If you take customers through a step-by-step process unlike your competition offers, you have a unique method—something customers can only experience at your business.

In the Your Competitive Advantages section of the worksheet, list your brand's unique methods or unique benefits. If you don't think your brand has a unique process, list how experiencing your brand differs from your competition. For example, do you have a particular way of doing things? How do you treat your customers differently? How is working with you different?

List as many unique methods or unique benefits you can think of. As usual, don't spend too much time agonizing over creating a long list. Instead, simply list the methods or processes that are important to your brand and business. If you can't think of any unique ways, that's okay too. Many companies won't have a unique method when starting out. Instead, they develop over time as they work with more customers or clients.

# Step 3
# Attracting Your Perfect Customers

———— ❧ ————

### Guiding Company Values

Your company values are a set of guidelines to start establishing your brand's point of view. A brand that doesn't have a set of values is like a car without a driver. It gets nowhere. You can think of your values as items on your brand's manifesto.

The best way to start listing your brand's values is to start taking a stand. Your brand doesn't have to take a stand on highly controversial topics like politics and religion. But it does need to stand for something. So what does your company stand for? What does it stand against?

Look at the products and services that your company offers or promotes. There were reasons you chose them over other options. Some of the reasons were because they benefited the company. Some other reasons were because they helped your customers. Take a stand for the reasons your products or services benefit your customers.

Your brand's core values influence the way your business operates—from the type of business you chose to the experience you give your customers. Writing them down makes them real and tangible to you and your team.

For example, here is the list of core values at Zappos.com:

1. Deliver WOW through service.
2. Embrace and drive change.
3. Create fun and a little weirdness.
4. Be adventurous, creative, and open-minded.
5. Pursue growth and learning.
6. Build open and honest relationships with communication.
7. Build a positive team and family spirit.
8. Do more with less.
9. Be passionate and determined.
10. Be humble.

Here are the core values for Southwest Airlines:

1. Work hard.
2. Desire to be the best.
3. Be courageous.

4. Display urgency.

5. Persevere.

6. Innovate.

7. Follow the golden rule.

8. Adhere to the basic principles.

9. Treat others with respect.

10. Put others first.

11. Be egalitarian.

12. Demonstrate proactive customer service.

13. Embrace the SWA family.

14. Have FUN.

15. Don't take yourself too seriously.

16. Maintain perspective.

17. Celebrate successes.

18. Enjoy your work.

19. Be a passionate team player.

Finally, here are the core values for The Honest Company:

1. Create a culture of honesty.

2. Make beauty.

3. Outperform.

4. Service matters.

5. Sustain life.

6. Be accessible.

7. Pay it forward.

8. Fun!

Now it's your turn! In the Your Brand's Guiding Values section of your worksheet, start listing your brand's core values. Don't spend more than thirty minutes on this task. You don't need to get a complete list of your brand's values. You only need enough to start establishing the culture and experience you want inside your brand.

**Your Magnetic Brand**

Let's talk about leveraging brand personality to attract your perfect customers. First, think of brand personality as how your brand shows up in the marketplace. Then what it says when it gets there. So your brand's personality is how your brand interacts with customers in real life and online.

Your company probably already has some personality. We need to define that personality and highlight it in your brand.

Business owners create a mission statement, brand values, or manifesto for their brand. But that's when they typically stop and miss out on opportunities to stand out. But that gives you the chance to build a memorable brand. Brand personality is an essential piece because it's critical for attracting the right customers.

You can showcase brand personality in all your company's marketing assets. You can inject personality into your business cards, in printed brochures, online ads, and more. You can use the same words and phrases your brand uses to make a statement.

Different people have different ways of saying the same thing. Your target audience may even have a vocabulary and phrases they use among themselves. For example, does your audience use "flawless," "on point," or "on fleek?"

After crafting your brand's personality, you can then determine how your brand uses words and phrases. You can choose the way it communicates the message ensuring the message sticks with the people hearing it and resonates with your audience.

**Five Dimensions of Brand Personality Traits**

In 1997, Jennifer Aaker published her framework on the five "Dimensions of Brand Personality." I have found this model to be a great starting point for designing a brand's personality. The five dimensions are:

- Sincerity
- Excitement
- Competence
- Sophistication
- Ruggedness

**Sincerity brands** are a "hometown" or "person next door" type of personality. They're the ones that are more friendly and approachable. Of course, every brand wants to be sincere, but Sincerity brands put it front and center.

Sincerity brands are genuine and honest brands. They're more family-friendly, small-town, or wholesome. They're friendly and cheerful brands, brightening your day with a smile and a kind hello.

Some examples of Sincerity brands are Campbell's, Amazon, Hallmark, and Disney.

**Excitement brands** are trendy cool brands. They are daring and spirited, living life to the fullest. They are unique and imaginative, refusing to conform to the rules of the establishment.

Excitement brands appeal to a more enthusiastic audience. They are daring, spirited, young (or young at heart), unique, and imaginative. They are daring to be different with a unique and high-octane style.

Some good examples of Excitement brands are Nike, Red Bull, TikTok, Monster Energy, and MTV.

**Competence brands** are dependable ones that know how to get the job done. They're confident, and they're hardworking, intelligent, and successful.

All the other brands may think they can do the job. But Competence brands are the ones you go to when you need the work done right. Think of Competence brands as reliable, leaders, technical, and secure.

Some good examples of Competence brands are VOLVO, Google, Intel, UPS, Chase, and Verizon.

**Sophistication brands** are stylish and glamorous brands. They follow the latest trends or define them. Sophistication brands are the ones that focus on the upper class. They're charming, and they're good-looking brands. They're the brands that operate at a level other brands dream of reaching but probably never will.

Being glamorous is about being sophisticated with a balance of glitz and pizzazz without looking cheap, ever. The same goes for Sophistication brands. Only the best will do for them and their customers.

Think of Sophistication brands as upper class, glamorous, charming, and good-looking. They never look cheap or tacky. And they only want what's best for their customers.

Some good examples of Sophistication brands are American Express, Mercedes, Apple, and Tiffany & Co.

**Ruggedness brands** are the tough, determined brands. They're the ones who don't mind getting dirty, and they enjoy the value of a hard day's work. So they're the outdoorsy brands. They are the rough, strong, and masculine brands.

They'd rather be outdoors rather than stuck inside of a cubicle. A rugged lifestyle demands toughness and determination. Ruggedness brands don't mind getting their hands dirty and respect the value of a hard day's work. So they're likely to run off on an adventure without a map or a plan. Then proudly track the mud into the house when they get back.

Some good examples of Ruggedness brands are Jeep, Harley-Davidson, REI, Levi's, and Jack Daniel's.

**Identify Your Competitions Personalities**

Which of the five personalities matches your competitors' brands?

Early on, you listed your top five direct competitors. So let's use that list and find out where there are opportunities in your market.

Back inside your worksheet, move to the Direct Competition's Brand Personality section. In the table, list the name of your direct competitor and what you think is the prominent personality of their brand. For example, is each competition a Sincerity, Sophistication, or Excitement brand? Are they more Ruggedness? Or are they more of a Competence brand?

Look at the logo, colors, and photography they are using in their marketing. You can trust your gut or first reaction to each of them. If you're still unsure, you can ask friends which personality the brand seems more like.

After identifying the personality for each of your direct competitor brands, look at the list of personalities. Do you notice any patterns? Many times you will find that your competition clusters around one to two personalities. Below the table in the worksheet, add notes on what you observe.

**Identify Your Customer Avatars Personalities**

Remember those customer avatars you created earlier? It's time to decide the leading personality for each of those. But we're going to do things a little different than we did with your direct competition.

People's personalities are complex with many dimensions. A pattern doesn't always appear with one personality. So pick two personalities for your customer avatars—a primary personality then a secondary one.

In the Customer Avatar's Personality section of the worksheet, add the first name of each customer avatar. Then decide which of the five personalities best matches the primary personality of each customer avatar.

Is one of your customer avatars more wholesome, friendly, cheerful, or family-oriented? **Sincerity** may be their primary personality trait.

Is one of your customer avatars more daring, spirited, unique, or independent?

**Excitement** may be their primary personality trait.

Is one of your customer avatars more reliable, hardworking, technical, or a leader?

**Competence** may be their primary personality trait.

Is one of your customer avatars more glamorous, charming, smooth, or upper class?

**Sophistication** may be their primary personality trait.

Is one of your customer avatars more outdoorsy, tough, rebellious, or disruptive?

**Ruggedness** may be their primary personality trait.

For each of your customer avatars, pick the primary personality trait from these five and add it to the worksheet's Customer Avatar's Personality section.

Next, pick the secondary personality trait for each of your customer avatars. You are choosing one of the four personalities that are different from their primary personality. In other words, you can't pick the same personality twice. Finally, add the secondary personality to each customer avatar in the worksheet's Customer Avatar's Personality section.

After every customer avatar has a primary and secondary personality, look at the table. Do you notice any patterns with the personalities of your customer avatars? Add your observations in the Notes section below the table in the worksheet.

**Pick Your Brand's Personality**

You've covered a lot of ground so far. You created your target customer avatars, identified your main competition, and explored both groups' personalities. Now you're ready to start making informed decisions about the design of your brand.

Every business owner wants their brand to stand out from the competition and create customer loyalty. The work you've done gives you the details you need to design a brand that will reach both of those goals. That's because you know the personalities of your market and can now see opportunities for your brand to thrive.

Your direct competitors are likely clustering around a personality or two. Likewise, your customer avatars probably have a few personalities in common. However, many times, the most common personality of your competitors and your avatars are not the same. That difference between your competitors and your avatars is your opportunity. The best chance for your brand is the personality that your avatars have in common—that your competitors aren't using.

For example, your competition may mostly have Competence brands. Your customer avatars tend to be more of a Sincerity personality. Of course, you could still design a brand with a Competence type of personality. But your brand will be more magnetic if you craft it to be a Sincerity type of personality.

Based on what you see in your competition and avatars, which personality type do you want for your brand? Pick the primary personality type for your brand. You can also choose a secondary personality type. Then add your brand's personality in the worksheet in the Your Brand's Personalities section.

For reference, here are the five personality types:

## Sincerity

Down-to-earth (family-oriented, small-town)

Honest (sincere, real)

Wholesome (original)

Cheerful (sentimental, friendly)

## Excitement

Daring (trendy, exciting)

Spirited (cool, young)

Imaginative (unique)

Up to date (independent, contemporary)

## Competence

Reliable (hardworking, secure)

Intelligent (technical, corporate)

Successful (leader, confident)

## Sophistication

Upper class (glamorous, good-looking)

Charming (feminine, smooth)

## Ruggedness

Outdoorsy (masculine, Western)

Tough (rebellious, combative, disruptive)

There are times when the personality of your avatars doesn't match your own personality. Don't feel like you need to force yourself into a brand personality that doesn't match yours. Authenticity is critical to the success of any brand. Instead, you'll use the personality trait that's already inside you.

The reality is that there you have each of the five personality traits at different times. You express those personality traits in your unique way. For example, Bear Grylls and Clint Eastwood have rugged personalities. But the way each of them is rugged is different.

The personality types you choose here for your brand are just the starting point.

Instead of creating something that isn't authentic, you're going to express that trait in your unique way. So, for example, your version of rugged is injected into the brand, especially if your business is a team of one (solopreneur) or you're designing a personal brand for yourself.

### Additional Personality Traits

You're a much more complex person than just one of those five personalities. So the next task is to add more personality traits to the worksheet. Add attributes that better define the unique personality of your brand.

You are no longer using the five personality traits here. Instead, you are adding whichever personality traits you want.

Let's say you chose the Sincerity brand, making your brand down to earth, honest, wholesome, and cheerful. But that probably doesn't encompass everything you want your company to stand for.

In the Additional Brand Personality Traits section of the worksheet, add more personality traits of your brand—characteristics that help explain your brand's personality to others. Thus making your brand more unique and helping it stand out. Add at least five new personality traits to the list in your worksheet.

To help, here are some personality traits you might use;

**48 Example Personality Traits**

| | |
|---|---|
| Adventurous | Focused |
| Ambitious | Friendly |
| Approachable | Independent |
| Articulate | Inexperienced |
| Autonomous | Inquisitive |
| Calm | Insightful |
| Charismatic | Intuitive |
| Clever | Meticulous |
| Competitive | Open-minded |
| Confident | Opinionated |
| Cooperative | Organized |
| Courteous | Patient |
| Creative | Perceptive |
| Curiosity | Persuasive |
| Debonair | Procedural |

| | |
|---|---|
| Determined | Protective |
| Devoted | Punctual |
| Diligent | Quiet |
| Educated | Relaxed |
| Efficient | Resourceful |
| Eloquent | Responsible |
| Energetic | Sporting |
| Enthusiastic | Talkative |
| Flexible | Technological |

**Brand Summary**

Now you have a better definition of the personality of your brand. That definition sets the direction in which you want to take your brand's design.

Next, in the Brand Summary of the worksheet, describe your brand in five words or less. You can write a complete sentence or just a series of descriptive words. Write whatever will help you summarize the brand to yourself and others.

## Creating a Magnetic Brand

You've already defined your brand's personality. Now it's time to make that personality magnetic using the law of attraction.

The law of attraction states that people who are similar to each other often attract one another. In business, it means that brands that are similar to their target customers often attract their target customers.

In other words, like attracts like.

Those perfect customers that like what your brand likes are part of your tribe. So out of your primary audiences, you're going to focus on attracting an even smaller subset. People fitting that smaller subset are members of your tribe. Let's start building that tribe.

But before you start, let me show you how focusing on your tribe helps you design your brand. Below, I've taken the Untapped Customers company name and designed logos for specific tribes.

Untapped Customers is my company that helps people grow their business online through education and consulting. Each of these logos is an example of directing the company brand to a specific tribe.

Suppose the brand's tribe were people that enjoyed buffalo wings, microbrews, and sports. Which logo would best fit that tribe?

If the brand's tribe were people that watch *Shark Tank*, read *TechCrunch*, and dream of building a startup, which logo would best fit that tribe?

When you clearly define your tribe, you can drive the design of your brand so that it speaks directly to them. Thus helping you get their attention quickly and build familiarity and trust faster.

### Create a Tribe Pinterest Board

You now have a better idea of who your tribe is. Create a new Pinterest board that represents your tribe. Typically I name the board (Company Name) + "tribe" such as "Untapped Customers Tribe." But you can name the board anything you want. Pin images to your Tribe board that represent brands that both your company and your tribe likes.

Pick one of your customer avatars and think about some of the brands they love. Then add those brands to your Tribe Pinterest board if your company likes them too.

For example, what clothing companies do your customer avatars use? Then add the logos and images of those brands to your Tribe Pinterest board.

Which specialty clothing stores do they like? Does your company like that brand too? If so, add the brand to your Tribe board.

What brand of shoes do your customer avatars like?

Which restaurants do they enjoy eating at?

Which snack or beverage brands do you both like?

What automotive brands do they like or prefer? Is there a particular vehicle they love?

Do they have any brands on their T-shirts or as bumper stickers?

Keep adding brands to your Tribe board on Pinterest. You can add and remove as many images as you need to the board. This board is all about curating the brand and pictures that you and your tribe love. This process is about using the law of attraction to position your brand and attract your perfect customers.

## Inspiration for Your Brand

You've looked at your competitions' brands and curated the brands your tribe likes. However, the missing piece is the style and inspiration for your brand. So create a third (and final) Pinterest board to gather inspiration for your brand. Typically I name the board (Company Name) + "inspiration," but you can name it whatever you want. You will be sharing this board with your designer, so keep this board public.

Before deciding how a brand looks, I first like to choose how a brand feels. You've selected the personality of your brand. Which materials, textures, or patterns match that personality? Is your brand more natural or organic? Or mathematical and precise? Start adding textures and patterns to your Inspiration Pinterest board.

Look at the textures and patterns that your tribe brands are using. Are there any you might want to use as inspiration for your brand?

Or perhaps there are other brands you like that aren't on your Tribe Pinterest board? Then add images of their patterns and textures to your Inspiration board.

For more inspiration, I like to explore stock imagery sites such as Creative Market. Simply go to creativemarket.com and search for textures and patterns that you like. For example, search for "Background texture" or "Background pattern" to see thousands of styles. You don't need to buy any images; you only need to pin them to your Inspiration Pinterest board.

Once you have a few backgrounds or patterns on your Pinterest board, start deciding your brand's style. Your first goal is to learn the name of the brand or style you want for your logo. I like to use creativemarket.com for that too. Go to creativemarket.com and search for "Logo template" products. Creative Market will show you thousands of different logo templates in lots of styles.

When you find a logo style you like, you can add it to your Inspiration Pinterest board. But also pay attention to the name of the template. The name will likely have keywords or phrases describing that logo style. Words such as "hand-drawn" or "minimal" or "retro."

Search creativemarket.com with keyword + "logo template" to find more logos with a similar style. For example, "Hand-drawn logo template" or "Minimal logo template" or "Retro logo template."

Continue paying attention to the names used to describe the style of your brand and logo. You're not going to use these logo templates. Instead, you're using them as inspiration and deciding what to call the style. Knowing the name of the style helps you more quickly discover more logos you'll like and helps you find designers.

Keep adding images of logos you like to your

Inspiration Pinterest board. You can also add photographs and images that help reinforce the style of your brand—whatever helps to clarify your brand and describe it to your designer.

There are other ways to find logos to add to your Inspiration board too. Google Images lets you search the entire web for logo inspiration. Visit images.google.com and search for your logo style + "logo examples." For example, "Minimal logo examples" or "Hand-drawn logo examples."

Pinterest will also recommend logos that are like the ones you pin to your board. You can add them to your board if you like any of the recommended pins.

Think of your Inspiration Pinterest board as a mood board for your brand. Add whatever images, logos, or photographs that help you visually show your brand's style.

Refer back to your Brand Competition and Tribe Pinterest boards from time to time. Is your brand's style in your Inspiration board different enough from the brands in your Brand Competition board? Does the style of your Inspiration board go with the style in your Tribe board?

It's okay if you start considering one style then start going in another direction. Don't forget that you're able to remove logo inspiration from your Pinterest board too. You can remove any pins from your board that no longer represent the direction of your brand.

Keep exploring and figuring out which direction you want for the design of your logo and brand. You can stop adding pins whenever you're happy with the contents of your brand's Inspiration Pinterest board. Then collect all the words you found that describe the style of logo you want. We will use that list of words later to help find the best designers for you.

**You're Ready to Design Your Logo!**

You've done all the exercises, and you have an excellent style direction for your brand.

You understand more about your competition, especially your direct competition. You have a plan of how your brand is going to stand out from the competition.

You defined the tribe your brand is attracting— the groups you're focusing on and speaking to with your branding. You then chose the personality of your brand and a style that will attract those perfect customers.

The three Pinterest boards you created are your reference to who you want to attract, where you want to stand out, and the inspiration of your new brand. In the next section, I'll explain how to take these three Pinterest boards and design your logo. Then later, I will show you how to create the rest of your brand.

# Magnetic Brand Method Part II
# Logo Design

———— ❧ ————

## Step 4
## Before Designing Your Logo

B efore you start designing your logo, there are a few things to know and understand.

A well-designed logo is simple, meaning it's not overly complex with too many design elements. Simple logos are easier to remember and recognize. Good logos are timeless. They aren't following the latest trends or fads—staying current and relevant as trends and fads fade away.

Your logo will appear in many different sizes and mediums. Your logo is used in the browser tab and several places on your website. It also needs to look good on smartphones and desktop computers. A good logo is versatile and multipurpose—recognizable at a wide range of sizes from tiny to large.

A good logo is unambiguous. It communicates one message, story, or metaphor. Your logo should not try to say too much visually. Don't try to cram different stories into one particular logo. Instead, focus on one primary metaphor or story to present in the logo. And keep the story within your logo short and to the point.

Your logo should be original. You've gathered a collection of inspiring logos from other brands. Part of the Magnetic Brand Method is to collect design inspiration to create a logo and brand that uniquely represents your company and its values.

### Black & White Logos

Your logo should look good in color and in black and white. I see lots of designers using colorful gradients in the logos they design. They look great in color, but will they look great in black and white?

Color won't always be an option for your logo. Sometimes you'll need to show it in a solid color or grayscale, for example, when being used in a book or newspaper. Sometimes you'll need a black and white version of your logo, such as when your logo is being screen printed onto pens or other marketing swag.

Imagine you wanted to get pens made with your logo to hand out. Logos on pens can only be one color. During the printing process, the barrel of the pen spins so multiple colors won't line up.

Now you may never be able to print your brand's logo on a pen. So you must use the black and white version of your logo. Design the black and white version along with the color version of your logo. Don't make the black and white version an afterthought.

The Instagram logo includes color gradients. The designers created a black and white version for the brand too. The black and white version is widely used on other websites when they link to their Instagram profile.

You will use the black and white version of your logo more often than you might think. Nearly all logo designers like to present only the color version of the logo to their clients. Ask to see the black and white version during the design process as well. Be sure they send you the black and white version of your logo as well as the color version.

## Exclusive vs. Nonexclusive Rights

Before paying for a logo, it's essential to understand the rights of what you're buying—especially the difference between exclusive and nonexclusive rights to a design.

With exclusive design rights, you, as the client, take full ownership of the logo design. The designer creates original artwork as your logo and sends it to you. When the project is complete, you take full legal ownership of the logo design. The designer cannot reuse or resell all or parts of your logo in future projects for other clients.

With nonexclusive design rights, you do not take full ownership of that logo design. The designer keeps the rights to the logo artwork. Designers are allowed to reuse the design on projects for other clients when they hold the rights.

For example, Creative Market has thousands of logo templates to buy with a nonexclusive license. When you buy a logo template from Creative Market, they can sell the same template to someone else.

Nonexclusive rights enable you to get a great logo design at a low price. But it also means that another company might exist with the same or similar logo as your brand. That's all because they can continue selling the same file to others.

If you want to ensure that no other company has the same logo as your brand, look for designers offering exclusive rights to their design clients. Expect to pay more for the design because the designer cannot resell or reuse the design.

Be sure to read the terms of what you're purchasing before buying a logo design. Understand whether you're buying exclusive or nonexclusive rights to a design before sending payment.

## License Agreements

If you are designing a brand for commercial projects, avoid legal headaches and don't use free images. When you buy an image from Creative Market or a stock image site, you are buying permission to use the artwork according to the license agreement with the purchase.

A licensing agreement is a legal contract where the owner of an image grants permission for its use to a person or company. It states that the original copyright owner retains ownership of the artwork.

It also details the terms on how, when, and where you, the licensee, can use it.

Read the license agreement before buying an image for your logo, website, or any other use in your business. Ensure the license agreement gives you the right to use the graphic in the manner you're considering. For example, some license agreements for icons don't allow you to use the icons in brand logos.

Designers can buy stock images to use in branding and design projects too. Whenever you hire a designer, be sure to ask if they used any third-party images as part of the project. If they did, ask the designer for the licensing information of the third party they used in the logo.

The designer can transfer some license agreements to you, but not all of them. If the license agreements are not transferable, buy the image through your company and send it to the designer to use. This way, the license is in your company's name.

**Raster vs. Vector Images**

Whether designing logos on your own or hiring a designer, you will be working with several image file formats. File formats such as EPS, JPG, SVG, TIFF, PNG, AI, and you might be thinking...

- What do these file extensions mean?
- When do I use each of these files?

Let's look at what each file format does and when you may want to use it in your marketing materials.

To start, some of the files are for digital materials, such as your website. Others are for print materials, such as your business cards. But there are two basic types of graphics files: raster and vector. Knowing the difference helps you pick the proper file format for the right job.

**Raster image files** are constructed of tiny squares called pixels. Each pixel is a solid color and, when put together, they create the image. The size of each pixel determines if a picture looks sharp or looks fuzzy.

The resolution of an image or device is based on the number of pixels per inch (or pixel density). The higher the pixel density, the sharper the picture looks. The lower the pixel density, the fuzzier the image looks. High-definition TVs look sharper than regular TVs because they have a higher pixel density.

The same goes for your logo. The higher the pixel density, the sharper the logo looks. When you make a raster logo bigger, you make the pixels bigger—lowering the resolution and making it look fuzzy.

Be careful when making a raster version of your logo bigger. Make it too big then you start to see the pixels. That's where vector versions of your logo can help!

**Vector image files** are created from mathematical lines and points, not pixels. Vector image files can be sized and scaled to any size without looking fuzzy, from a tiny dot to the size of a billboard. When you make a vector image bigger, you make the lines and points bigger before the pixels are colored.

**So which file formats are raster and which are vector?**

The most common raster logo file formats are JPG, PNG, GIF, and TIFF. The most common vector logo file formats are EPS, PDF, SVG, and

AI. If you're sending your logo to a designer, send them the vector file formats.

Beware when working on your own; vector files CAN contain raster images. Whenever a vector file contains raster images, treat it like a raster image. Changing the file extension does not convert it from raster to vector (or vice versa).

**Here are some tips for using your logo files:**

#1 Use the vector version of your logo whenever you can.

#2 The raster version of your logo can become smaller but not bigger.

#3 You can create a raster version of your logo from a vector file when you need to.

**Typefaces, Fonts, and More**

As a brand owner, you will hear about font families, typefaces, and fonts. A font family, typeface, and font are different from each other but related. Understanding the difference between them will help you make better design decisions.

When a designer creates a font, each character in a language is designed one at a time. Each character is designed with the same style and thickness to match the other characters. The collection of letters, characters, and punctuation is called a typeface.

**Typeface:** A specific design of text characters.

The letter designs are then combined in a file to create a font.

**Font:** A set of characters in a specific weight, style, orientation, and width.

When a designer wants to design two different weights in the same style, they need to create two fonts, such as a Regular font, an Italic font, and or a Bold font. Perhaps even a Light font. Those different fonts are combined to create a font family.

**Font Family:** A group of related fonts with a similar design but different weight, orientation, and width.

When a designer wants to design different text styles that go well together, they put two or more typefaces together to create a superfamily.

**Font Superfamily:** A group of font families that fall into different classifications.

Roboto on Google Fonts is an excellent example

to learn from. Search for Roboto on Google Fonts. (fonts.google.com)

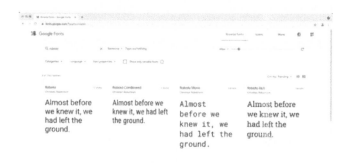

You'll see different Roboto styles, including Roboto Condensed, Roboto Mono, and Roboto Slab. Roboto is the font superfamily. Roboto Condensed is a font family. Roboto Mono is another font family.

The Roboto Condensed font family consists of six different Roboto fonts, including Light, Regular, Italic, and Bold.

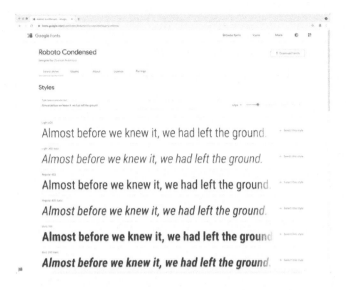

Think of the font as the file on your computer. The typeface is the design of the characters inside the font file. A font family is a suite of font files. A font superfamily is a collection of font families that have a design style in common. This knowledge will come in handy when picking the typefaces and fonts for your brand.

**Avoid Distorting Text**

Avoid distorting, stretching, or squishing text. There have been many times when I wanted a wider or thinner version of a font for a design. Font designers spend a lot of time making sure each letter looks good and works well. Distorting the shapes of letters makes them harder to read because you're lowering the integrity of the design of the letters. Instead, use a wide or condensed version of typeface. If it's a logo design, you might also try adding more or less space between the letters.

**Color Psychology**

Earlier, you started defining the personality of your brand. You picked one of the five main areas that added in other personality traits. You can use color psychology to reinforce that personality. You can also choose the main color for your logo based on the emotions associated with that color.

Here are some of the emotions associated with different colors:

- Red: Excitement, bold, and youthful.
- Orange: Friendly, cheerful, and confident.
- Yellow: Optimism, warmth, and clarity.
- Green: Peaceful, health, and growth.
- Blue: Trust, strong, and dependable.
- Purple: Creative, wise, and imaginative.
- Gray: Balance, calm, and neutral.

Revisit your Brand Competition Pinterest board. Which color are your competitor brands using as the main color in their logos? Using a different main color from your competition is a great way to stand out. Choose a different color that has emotions matching the personality of your brand.

## The Six Types of Logos

Logo design is an essential element of any company's branding. But your brand's logo can be more than just typing your company name in a font and picking a color.

A logo is a vital piece of a company's identity. It should communicate the company's core values and be both memorable and relevant.

Did you know that you can use more than one logo in your brand? Here are the six types of logos you should know about:

## Brand Mark, Pictorial Mark, or Symbol Icon

Brand marks are called many different names for the same thing. While the typeface is for a company's brand name, the brand mark is how people recognize the brand. The ultimate goal for a major brand is for the brand mark to become so well known that it can stand on its own.

Think of how Apple only uses its brand mark on its computers and phones, without its name. Or how

Starbucks uses only its brand mark on the cups. And think of the brand marks used as app icons.

When creating brand marks for your brand, it's usually better to represent the story or the metaphor instead of being too literal or too representative of your product or services. For example, Apple's brand mark isn't a computer or a phone. Starbucks' brand mark isn't a cup of coffee. Not being literal gives them the ability to create new products or services without changing the logo. Not changing the logo helps to reinforce the message or story behind the brand.

Some well-known examples of brand mark logos are:

1. Nike's Swoosh logo.
2. Apple's apple logo.
3. Snapchat's ghost logo.
4. The Rolling Stones' lips logo.
5. Twitter's bird logo.
6. Target's bullseye logo.

**Mascots**

Mascots are a type of logo that typically represents a company, organization, or team through an animal or character. Mascots can be a terrific way for your brand to build a rapport with your ideal customers. Plus, they're just plain fun!

Some well-known examples of mascot logos are:

1.  Tony the Tiger.
2.  The Colonel from KFC.
3.  Mr. Peanut.
4.  The Pillsbury Doughboy.
5.  The Burger King.
6.  Mr. Clean.

## Wordmarks

Wordmark logos are simply the company name presented in a specific typestyle and presentation. Typography is an important decision as the focus will be on your company's name. Pick a font that represents the personality of your brand. Don't stop at only typing your company name. Customize or modify your wordmark to make it unique and stand out.

Some well-known examples of wordmark logos are:

1.  Visa
2.  Google

3. Coca-Cola
4. eBay
5. FedEx
6. Amazon

## Monograms or Lettermarks

Monogram logos are logos that consist of letters, usually brand initials in a decorative design. If your brand's name is long or confusing, a monogram may be the best option for a logo. They work well in global markets. They're also a smart choice for companies with long or difficult to pronounce names. For example, NASA is just an abbreviation for National Aeronautics and Space Administration.

When designing a monogram logo, use a distinct typeface that matches your brand's personality. Play and experiment with the shapes and layout of the letters. Try removing parts of the letters or letting the letters interlock with each other. Have the letters work together to create a symbol that represents your brand.

Some well-known examples of monogram logos are:

1.  Louis Vuitton
2.  Channel
3.  New York Yankees
4.  HP (Hewlett-Packard)
5.  3M
6.  GE (General Electric)

## Emblems or Badges

An emblem logo consists of text inside of a symbol or icon. Think badges, seals, and crests. These logos are often the go-to choice for schools, organizations, or government agencies because they have a traditional and striking appearance.

Emblem logos are a modern take on the traditional logo, many times with a touch of originality. They encapsulate design features within an elegant frame or border. Emblem logos are an excellent choice for brands that want to have a touch of time-honored tradition or nostalgia.

Some well-known examples of monogram logos are:

1.  Harvard crest
2.  Harry Potter school and house crests
3.  NFL logo
4.  Harley-Davidson logo

5. BMW logo

6. Superman logo

## Combination Logos

As the name suggests, a combination mark is a logo that incorporates two of the other logotypes together. Each logotype in the combination can also stand alone, allowing for more flexibility with the brand's identity.

The most common form of a combination logo is a brand mark combined with a wordmark. Chase Bank, for example, has its octagon symbol and its Chase wordmark. Sometimes the two marks are combined to create their combination logo. But each logotype can be used on its own as well.

Some well-known examples of combination logos are:

1. Taco Bell

2. Microsoft

3. Puma

4. PayPal

5. Walmart

6. Adidas

## How many logos should a company have?

The answer isn't straightforward, especially for smaller companies. Much of it depends on where and how you will use your logos. At a minimum, your brand will need a wordmark. It's also common to design a brand mark for your brand. Then you can create a combination logo using the wordmark and brand mark.

If I know the brand will last a year or more, I like to adopt a responsive logo approach. Responsive logos are the same logo designed in different sizes, complexity, or even color to accommodate and adapt to its use. Regardless of the variation, it will still be recognizable as belonging to the company it represents.

For example, your brand will have the logo at the top of the pages on a website. But it should also have a favicon. A favicon is a tiny icon that appears in the browser tab when people visit your website. Favicons can be as small as 16x16 pixels but are usually 32x32 pixels, so they don't give you much room for a highly detailed logo or icon.

For new brands, I will usually create a wordmark and a brand mark. Then put the two together into a vertically orientated combination logo and a horizontally oriented combination logo. I will then create a simpler version of the brand mark to use as the favicon—giving the brand a lot of flexibility and ensuring the brand is represented well at nearly all sizes.

# Step 5
# Designing Logos on Your Own

———— ❧ ————

A dobe Illustrator is the most advanced tool you can use for designing logos. It's the tool used by most logo designers. Since it's an advanced tool, however, that means it can be challenging to learn. Fortunately, alternative options are available for you to use instead.

Suppose you want to design a logo for your brand on your own. In that case, there are two options I recommend: use a vector editing tool or use a logo generator. Google Drawings is a vector editing tool that you can use.

For an updated list of other vector editing tools, visit the following web address:

branddesignsecrets.com/resources

Google Drive is available at drive.google.com and is free to use with any Gmail account, such as your Gmail or YouTube account. To start designing a new logo for your company, log in to Google Drive. Click the New button in the top left. Then under the "More" option, choose Google Drawings. Google Drawings will open with a blank canvas.

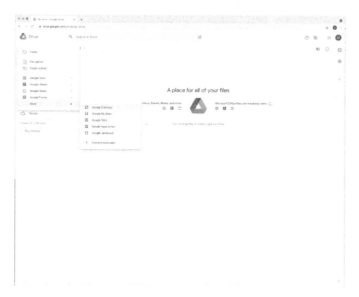

**Design a Wordmark Logo**

First, give your Google Drawings file a name such as (brand name) + "wordmark." Then you're ready to design a wordmark logo for your brand. Start creating a wordmark logo by selecting the text tool. Then click anywhere to add a text box to the canvas. Type the name of the company and select all the text in the box. Now it's time to choose a font for your wordmark logo.

Google offers a wide variety of fonts for free in

a separate project called Google Fonts. Google has loaded all those fonts into Google Drawings for you to use. In a new tab or browser window, visit fonts.google.com to see all the fonts you can use. Most of the fonts have different weights, such as Light, Regular, and Bold. So be sure to view a font you think might work and find the perfect thickness of the letters for your wordmark.

Uncertain which font to use in your wordmark? I share some of my favorite Google fonts at:

branddesignsecrets.com/resources

Type your brand's name in the preview text field to see what your wordmark would look like. Find a font you think best matches the personality you chose for your brand. Make a note of the name of the font and go back to Google Drawings.

Back in Google Drawings, make sure you have the text box selected (the one that has the name of your brand in it). At the top of the page, open the Font selection menu. Google Drawings will show you a list of popular Google fonts.

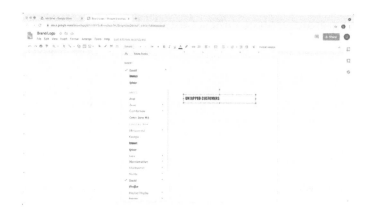

Look to see if the font you picked earlier is on the list. If it's not, then click 'More fonts' and search for the name. Then click on the font name to change the text in the box to that font.

**Congratulations, you created a wordmark logo for your brand!**

Don't worry about picking a color for your logo just yet. Leave the wordmark black for now. Later on, I will show you how to create a color scheme. Then you can pick one of the colors for your logo.

**Add a Brand Mark Logo**

You could use the shapes in Google Drawings to create a brand mark. But Google Drawings is limited, and the process will likely be time-consuming and frustrating. Instead, I recommend buying a brand mark from logo markets such as

LogoGround. Look for brand marks that don't contain words or have words that can be removed and look good.

I keep an updated list of where you can buy exclusive and nonexclusive brand marks at:

branddesignsecrets.com/resources

When shopping or designing a brand mark, remember, it's more interesting if the brand mark communicates a story or metaphor. Don't be too literal or too representative of your product or services. For example, if you're designing a brand for a coffee shop, creating a brand mark with a coffee mug can be expected and uninteresting. You could use a brand mark with a coffee mug but make sure the design you choose is attractive somehow. Also, be sure the style of the brand mark you select matches your brand's personality.

If you find a brand mark you love but doesn't quite match your brand's personality, explore adjusting your brand's personality. The marks and personality you choose for your brand are up to you. But everything needs to be in alignment with each other.

After you have found a great brand mark for

your logo, download it as a vector file (i.e., .eps, .ai, or .svg file extensions). Google Drawings only works with the EMF file format for vector images. So we will need to convert your brand mark to the EMF format using CloudConvert.

In a new tab or browser window, go to the cloudconvert.com web address. After CloudConvert loads, select the brand mark file from your computer to upload and convert. Under the "Convert to..." option, find and choose the EMF file format. Then click the "Convert" button to change the file to that format. Once the file has converted, download the .emf file to your computer. Then upload the .emf file to Google Drive.

After uploading the file to Google Drive, you can open it in Google Drawings. To do that, right-click on the file in Google Drive. Then under the "Open with..." menu option, choose Google Drawings. Your brand mark image will open in a new Google Drawings document. Give this new Google Drawings document a name, such as (brand name) + "brand mark."

## Congratulations, you created a brand mark logo for your brand!

Adjust the brand mark to your liking. You can add or remove shapes. You can move pieces around. Make whatever changes you want to the brand mark. Keep the brand mark black or grayscale for now. Like the wordmark logo, you can change the colors of your brand mark after you pick your color scheme.

### Create Brand Combination Logos

Put your brand mark and wordmark logos together to form the combination logos of your brand.

To start, make both marks the same height in the horizontal combination logo. Then place the brand mark to the left of the wordmark. For the vertical version, make both marks the same width. A good starting place between the two marks is 5%, 10%, or 12.5% of the brand mark width for horizontal logos. For vertical logos, try setting the space between 5%, 10%, or 12.5% of the height of the brand mark.

These guidelines for the sizing and spacing of your combination logos are just starting points. Logo design is more art than science. If a combination looks right but doesn't follow the mathematical rules, that's okay. The logos need to look good and be easy for people to interpret.

I have created a Google Drawings document with some grids to help guide the spacing and size of your combination logos. It's available with many other book resources at:

branddesignsecrets.com/resources

Save the Logo Grids file to your Google Drive. Then open the files for your brand mark and wordmark logos with Google Drawings. Copy and paste each of the logos into the Logo Grids document. Align your brand mark and wordmark logos on the grid as shown in the sample logos.

The Logo Grids file contains multiple examples of horizontal and vertical logos. Typically you will only need one horizontal and vertical version of your combination logos to start. You can create more if you need to.

**Congratulations, you've created the combination logos for your brand!**

After creating all the combination logos your brand needs, delete the grids and example logos.

**Exporting Logos from Google Drawings**

All the logos for your brand are currently in a single Google Drawings file. You will need to create separate files for each version of your logo before exporting your logos. Open the File menu in Google Drawings and click "Make a copy" to make a new copy of the current document.

Give the new document a different name such as (brand name) + "horizontal logo" or (brand name) + "vertical logo."

In the new document, delete all other graphics except for the logo you want to keep. For example, if you are working in the horizontal logo version, delete everything except your horiz

Next, drag and select all the parts of the combination logo. With everything selected, open the Arrange menu and select "Group." Grouping will keep everything together whenever you move them. Plus, it makes it easier to select everything in the group.

Google Drawings doesn't automatically crop images when you export them. You will need to reduce the amount of unused space around the logo yourself. Move the logo to the top left of the canvas. (It's okay if they are touching the top and left sides.)

Grab the handle in the bottom right corner of the canvas and drag it close to your logo, but not touching it. Google Drawings will likely adjust your view of the document, zooming in to the logo.

Select the logo, then click and drag it to the middle of the canvas. You can make the space around the logo as large or small as you like. But make sure that none of the edges of the logo are touching the edges of the canvas.

As mentioned earlier, you will want some raster versions along with some vector versions. In Google Drawings, open the File menu, then open the Download sub-menu and select a file format. Google Drawings will show you several file formats for downloading your logo file: PDF (.pdf), JPEG (.jpg), PNG (.png), and SVG (.svg).

Download your logo in each of the following formats: JPG, PNG, and SVG. The JPG image will automatically have a white background. The PNG image will have a transparent background. The SVG file is the vector version of your logo.

You may later realize that you need a larger version of your logo's JPG or PNG versions. If so, you will need to make the size of your canvas bigger then increase the size of the logo. You can then download the image in JPG or PNG format at a bigger size.

I recommend making copies of your logo files each time you make a new version of your logo. For example, say you need to make a version of your logo that is all white. Make a copy of your logo file, THEN make the changes. This way, you have the original file available in case you need to use it again. Choose a naming convention and file organization system that works for you.

## Designing with Logo Generators

If drawing your logo seems overwhelming, a logo generator might be a good option. Many logo generators are free, but there are some paid versions too. Beware, some logo generators don't let you know they require payment until after you have designed a logo. Others will let you download a JPG or PNG version of your logo but charge you to download the vector version. Find out about the pricing for a logo generator before spending time using one.

In general, the brand marks are provided or sold using nonexclusive agreements. In other words, the brand mark will likely not be unique to your company. But your wordmark will be special because it's your brand's name in a particular font style.

Logo generators will ask you to provide the name of your company and answer a few questions. They will then show you some logos to choose from, such as the industry or type of company the logo is for. Some will even let you make changes to the logo.

Some logo generators will ask you to choose different styles that you like. Use your Inspiration Pinterest board as a reference. Choose the logo styles that best match the direction you envisioned for your brand.

If a logo generator asks you to choose colors for your logo, refer back to your Inspiration and Tribe Pinterest boards. You may also want to refer back to the information about color psychology. Is there a particular energy that you want your brand to evoke? Or is there a logo color that might help you stand out from your competition?

A few logo generators will ask you for a slogan for the company. What you type in for the company slogan won't affect the style of the logo. Instead, they ask the question so they can add the slogan to the logo. I recommend not adding a slogan to your logo or create a version of the logo without the slogan. There will be very few times when you will need the slogan as part of the logo. But it might be helpful to have a slogan designed to match the logo.

I keep an updated list of logo generators available for you at:

branddesignsecrets.com/resources

Logo generators are handy for when you need a quick logo to get your brand off the ground—

especially when you're okay with another company having a similar logo. Then you can invest in a custom logo created by a logo designer at a later stage in your business.

# Step 6
# Hiring Logo Designers

———— ❧ ————

There is a lot of confusion and mystery around hiring a designer to create a logo for your brand. Finding the right designer can be overwhelming. After all, no one wants to pay money for a logo that they aren't happy with. Let's go through some things you should know about the process before looking for a designer.

Before hiring a designer, I recommend determining your logo design budget and what rights you're looking for. You can find logo designers ranging from as little as $39 to millions of dollars for logo designs. Most of what you're paying for is the designer's time brainstorming ideas with you and creating the logo.

## Logo Design Templates

Logo design templates are sold with nonexclusive rights, so another business may have a logo very similar to yours. You discovered logo templates during your search in Creative Market. As you saw, there are thousands of logo templates available.

You could find a logo template you like, then hire a professional to help turn it into a logo for your brand. Logos designed from a template typically cost between $39 and $150. If you already found a logo template you like, you just need a freelance logo designer or graphic designer. You can find them on Upwork (upwork.com) or Fiverr (fiverr.com) to help you. Look at the designer's reviews to find a good quality designer.

**Custom Logo Design**

Instead of using a template, you could hire a designer to create a custom logo for your brand. The cost of custom designs typically ranges between $150 and $1000. Many agencies can create a custom logo for less than $300. The high-quality logo designers you find on Instagram or Dribbble will usually charge between $500 and $1,000.

The prices for custom logos vary wildly. You're mostly paying for the designer's time, including time to explore lots of options and create actual logos. There's a lot happening behind the scenes.

Good logo designers will let you know how much they charge early on in the logo design process. They should also let you see the design process, so you know what to expect. The only surprise for you in the logo design process should happen when they reveal what they've created for you.

Before hiring a designer for a custom logo, understand if you will be getting exclusive or nonexclusive rights to the artwork. If you come across a logo designer charging a lower price, understand why their rate is lower than others. It may be because they are using templates, or they are not selling you exclusive rights to their designs.

**Logo Designers Are Artists**

When looking for a logo designer to hire, it's important to remember that designers are artists. Not all designers master all logo styles. Instead, each designer will have styles they are great at while other styles are just okay, primarily because of the styles and industries they work in the most.

Logo designers start their careers designing logos in many styles for any company to get the experience. They might work for smaller design agencies or participate in logo design contests to gain experience. Over time, their portfolio will start to show styles in which they excel. Clever designers eventually begin specializing in the styles they are good at and carve a niche for themselves in the industry.

One of the best questions to ask yourself when reviewing a logo designer's portfolio is: "How good is this designer at the design style I want for my logo?" Finding a designer that specializes in designing logos in your style helps ensure the project will be successful.

When you ask a designer to create a style they aren't used to, it may be a challenging project for both of you. The designer will naturally bring in elements from the style they're used to, which could be good or bad. It all depends on the direction you want for your brand.

I enjoy HGTV home remodeling shows, probably too much. I especially enjoyed the show *Fixer Upper*. Joanna Gaines has an excellent eye for interior design. Over time, she started niching down to the farmhouse chic design style, becoming the go-to designer for that style.

A couple hired her to design their house in a mid-century modern/minimalist style in one episode. The house she designed looked great. But you could see elements of the farmhouse style she added into the house. The result wasn't what the couple could have gotten if they hired a designer specializing in mid-century modern or minimalist design. Instead, the result was a mid-century modern/minimalist house with hints of farmhouse chic.

The same goes for hiring a logo designer. If you want a logo for your brand in one specific style, look for designers specializing in that style. If you want your logo to pull influence from different styles, look for designers with experience in those styles.

Use your Pinterest board as a reference when comparing portfolios from one designer to another. For finding designers to hire, you have a lot of options of where to find them.

**Finding a Designer to Hire**

Where to go to find the right logo designer to hire depends largely on your budget.

If you're looking for a logo in the $39–$150 price range, Fiverr (fiverr.com), Upwork (upwork.com), and Etsy (etsy.com) are good places to start.

Upwork and Fiverr are both gig sites for people with all sorts of experience and expertise. You can find professional developers, social media marketers, copywriters, and of course, logo designers. Both sites have a wide variety of logo designers that you can hire directly. Fiverr lists logo designers under the Graphics and Design category.

Designers on Upwork and Fiverr offer different logo design packages. The designers get to pick what to include in each design package. Many packages include other design services, such as social media graphics or stationery design.

Remember, you always want to receive the vector version of your logo. But sometimes, they get tricky and don't include vector versions of the logo in some packages. If you buy a package without the vector logo, you cannot make the logo bigger, only smaller. This limitation might cause problems later on down the road.

For example, a logo designer may offer three

different packages: starter, standard and advanced. But the starter package doesn't include the vector files. Then don't buy the starter package. Instead, buy the standard or advanced package that includes the vector file.

After finding a quality designer, pick the package that best fits your needs.

Did you know you can find logo designers on Etsy (etsy.com)? It surprised me because I think of Etsy as the place for handmade and vintage craft items. But Etsy has a large number of logo designers, ranging from template to custom logo designers. Search Etsy for "Custom logo design" + (logo style) to find logo designers that might be a good fit for you.

If you're willing to pay $500–$1,000 (or more) for a logo design, Dribbble (dribbble.com) and Bēhance (behance.net) are where you find the higher-end designers.

Dribbble and Bēhance are portfolio sites for all types of designers, including graphic designers, video designers, web designers, and more. Search either of these websites for "logo," "identity," or "brand" to find logo designers.

Look at the designer's About page to see their design portfolio. If you like what you see, there will usually be a way for you to contact them and find out about working with them on your logo project. You usually won't need to sign up for an account at Dribbble or Bēhance to contact the designers. Many designers include links to their websites and social profiles, meaning you can contact them through their website, email address, or social media account. If the designer doesn't include those links, you will need to sign up for a free account to contact them.

## Searching for Logo Designers

If you cannot find the right designer from those options, you can find designers on Instagram. Search Instagram with the hashtags #logodesigner or #branddesigner. You can also search Instagram for (logo style) + "logo designer."

Look for a logo designer who matches the style you're looking for in your brand. When you find a designer, you can message them directly through Instagram. Their bio link will usually give you information about working with them, their design process, and maybe pricing.

Of course, your other option is to search on Google (or another search engine) to find logo designers. Just do a custom logo design search or whatever style you're looking for. I have found that searching for "Custom logo design" + (style) is a good search term to start with.

## Logo Design Agencies

If looking for a logo designer seems a bit daunting, there are logo agencies you can hire. These agencies have a variety of designers on their teams. Often hiring a logo design agency is more manageable than hunting the right designer. When you hire a logo agency, they will pick the best designer on their team to help you with your brand.

Many logo design agencies offer different logo design packages at different prices for you to choose from. Packages typically start at $199 for just a logo, including the vector versions. The larger packages will usually include additional services such as stationery design or social media graphics.

## Logo Design Contests

Your brand is more than just a logo. But your logo and brand must be in alignment to get attention. The design of the logo heavily influences the design direction of your brand image. Design contests, such as 99designs, are attractive to business owners who don't know what they want, allowing designers to determine the direction of their brand. Fortunately, that's not you.

You already gained clarity on the direction you want to take your brand. You also understand the market opportunities for your brand. This knowledge gives you the ability to hire the perfect designer while also saving you hundr

Design contests typically cost more than hiring designers or agencies. Logo contests on 99designs, for example, start at $299. That price is already higher than many logo design agencies (typically starting at $199). During the order process, they reveal that $299 is for the lowest level package.

Putting the numbers aside, I am honestly not a fan of design contests. Attracting mid or top-level designers costs $899 or more on 99designs! That's around the same price that many of the top designers on Dribbble and Bēhance charge.

The incentives of a design contest don't encourage participation by great designers. Consider them from the designers' perspective for a moment. Design contests force designers to invest their time and effort with no guarantee of winning the prize. Many will enter, only one will win.

Imagine working your job as part of a contest. Every day you competed against other people to see who gets picked as the winner and gets paid. If you lose, you don't get paid.

How often would you work that type of job?

How much time would you spend working on projects on that job?

How likely are you to choose that type of job instead of one that guarantees you will get paid for the work you do?

Because of the incentive structure, it's difficult for design contests to attract talented designers and keep them.

You know what you want and need in a brand because you're following the steps in this book. So I recommend avoiding design contests. Instead, find a designer or agency that can deliver what you're looking for.

## Tips When Hiring Designers or Agencies

Contact them before sending them a payment. Ask questions and see if they respond promptly. Make sure they are the right fit for you and that you'll enjoy working with them.

Share your Pinterest boards with them. Let them see the design inspiration you've gathered to help them know where you want to take your brand.

See my latest recommendations on finding good logo designers and agencies at:

branddesignsecrets.com/resources

## Logo Design Process

You need to be aware of the stages of the logo design process to know what to expect and make the process easier for everyone. Many designers will outline or describe their logo design process on their sales page. But sometimes, the language they use has a lot of technical jargon when explaining their process.

Designing a logo for your brand takes time, something you and the designers can never get back. But you don't want to pay for something you don't like. Most designers require at least a 50%

deposit before they start working on your logo. This way, they know you are serious about completing the project. You will then pay the remaining balance at the end of the project.

The contract or agreement between you and the designer should detail the payment structure. It should explain what happens if you or the designer terminate the contract before the end of the project. It should also mention who takes ownership of the artwork at the end of the contract. Make sure you understand the details of the contract and the payment structure before sending money to the designer.

At the start of the project, the logo designer will start brainstorming ideas for your brand's new logo. They'll pull inspiration from your Pinterest boards and explore a lot of ideas. It's normal for a logo designer to create twenty to thirty different ideas.

They will then narrow all those ideas down to a few initial concepts or design ideas. Most will be based on your request and your Pinterest boards. They may, however, include one or two "Out of the box" concepts based on something they discovered along the way.

The designer will refine each concept, but they will not be perfect. These initial concepts are usually very different ideas from each other. The goal at the initial concept stage is not to find the final logo. Instead, the goal is for the designer to learn which direction you want them to keep moving.

When the initial concepts are ready, the designer will send them to you for your feedback. Let the designer know which logo idea you like the best, along with any feedback you may have about the logo. Sending your feedback on the ideas completes the initial concept stage. The project then move

Iterations or revisions are the number of times you get to review logos and give the designer feedback. The designer will then make changes to the logo based on your feedback. Some designers offer unlimited revisions, and others limit the number you can have. The revisions will continue until you are happy with the logo or have reached your limit.

Send the remaining balance owed to the designer when the revisions are complete.

After the designer receives the payment, they will send you the logo files. Once you receive the files, the design project is complete. Then you get to start using your new logo!

## After Hiring a Logo Designer

Here are some valuable tips after hiring a designer to ensure your logo design project is successful.

### Send the designer the link to your three Pinterest boards.

You don't have to send them just your Inspiration Pinterest board. You can send them your Brand Competition and Tribe boards too. Explain the Pinterest boards to them and make sure they understand how they can help.

### Give honest and constructive feedback on the logo designs.

Don't feel like you need to hold back to prevent making the logo designer feel bad. They need your honest feedback at every stage. But keep your feedback helpful and constructive to get a logo you're proud of. Let the designer know what you like and don't like about each design.

**Don't give only solutions in your feedback.**

You and the designer have different experiences and backgrounds than each other. Leverage their knowledge during the process, especially when you can only communicate with the designer through messaging or email. Instead of only telling the designer what to fix, let them know the problems you see as well. Then together, you and the designer can explore ways to solve the problems. Offer suggestions, but make sure you're offering them the flexibility to explore on their own and try different ideas.

**Ask about third-party licenses.**

During the concept and iteration phases, ask if they used any third-party artwork in the design. If they did use images from a third party, ask where they got the images from. Then review the license agreement to make sure you can use the image as a logo before moving forward with the project.

**Logos from Your Designer**

You've just finished the process of ordering a logo and finally paid your designer. The designer will then send you several different logo files. You should receive your new logo in at least one vector format (.eps, .ai, .svg). You should also receive your logo in a raster format with a transparent background (.png or .tiff). If you are missing one of these files, ask your designer to send them to you.

Open each of the logo files to make sure everything looks good. Let the designer know if everything is okay or if there are any issues with the logo files. You can then post an honest review of your experience of working with the designer. Please post a review on the site where you found them or ask the designer where to leave your feedback.

## Organize and Back Up Your Logo Files

Organize the files in a way that works for you. You will use your logo files more often than you might think—creating graphics for social media, your website, marketing pages, and so on. I recommend making backup copies of your logo files in case something happens to your computer.

You're now ready to turn your logos into a brand!

# Magnetic Brand Method Part III
# Brand Kit Design

❖

## Step 7
## Your Brand Board

Looking at your logo on your computer and fonts in your browser window may give you a sense of whether they'll work together. But you won't be sure until you try them together. Creating a Brand board puts the different parts of your brand onto one page. Thus letting you see everything working together and whether you need to make adjustments.

Download or make a copy of the Brand board from the resources by visiting the following web address:

branddesignsecrets.com/resources

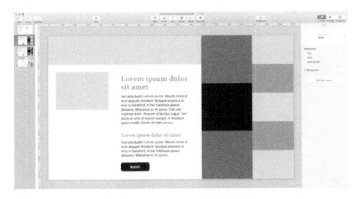

Open the Brand board template in Google Slides, PowerPoint, or Keynote. Add your logo on the left side of the slide, to the left of the text. The PNG or JPG version of the logo with a transparent or white background will work the best.

Add photos, illustrations, or textures to the Brand board presentation representing your brand's visual style. Save the brand presentation. You will continue to update it as you add pieces to your brand.

# Step 8
# Brand Fonts

———— ❧ ————

ypography plays a significant role in conveying the overall personality of a brand. It's a crucial element in creating your brand's identity and the way you present your company. The style of the typefaces you choose for your brand is an integral part of your business identity. It should fit with your logo and brand image and express the unique personality of your brand.

## Getting Your Brand Fonts

Before diving into how to choose the font families for your brand, there are some details you need to know. Here's what you must know about getting the font files and permission to use them in your marketing materials.

Google Fonts (fonts.google.com) has thousands of fonts available that you can use for free. In addition, you can use these fonts freely in your products and projects—they are royalty-free. (This isn't legal advice, so please consult a lawyer for full license details.)

Adobe also has a font service called Adobe Fonts that gives you access to thousands of fonts. Adobe Fonts is included with a Creative Cloud subscription (creativecloud.adobe.com) which means it's not free. But it does give you access to an extensive library of fonts and unlimited page views if you use the fonts on your website.

You can also buy fonts from a digital marketplace, such as Creative Market, for a one-time fee. The prices vary for each font. You may also need to purchase different licenses to use the font on your computer, on your website, or in an app. Using the font on your website may have a page view limit—for example, 10,000 page views per month or 100,000 page views per month. When your website traffic passes the limit, you need to buy a different license.

Lastly, you can buy fonts directly from the font designers. As with digital marketplaces, it's usually a one-time fee. You might need to purchase different licenses to use the font in different places like apps and websites. There may be restrictions on the number of page views too.

Many popular design applications include Google Fonts in their services such as Canva, Wave.video, and RelayThat. I always select two font families from Google Fonts for a brand kit I create because so many web applications use them. But those Google Fonts are not always the main brand fonts. Sometimes the Google Fonts are just the alternative fonts to use when I can't use the main ones.

Picking suitable font families is a balance of budget and style. If I cannot find the perfect font families for a brand on Google Fonts, I will typically look on Adobe Fonts next. If I don't see font families I like on Adobe Font, I will start looking at the digital marketplaces.

For an updated list of places to buy quality fonts for your brand, visit the web address below:

branddesignsecrets.com/resources

**Pairing Fonts for Visual Interest**

Making sure your brand's fonts go well together is a skill anyone can learn. The right typeface for your design can make all the difference in the visual impact of your brand! You can use the same font family for both, but it's not as interesting.

It's kind of like cooking. You could create a dish that is only sweet or only spicy, but it could become too much of a good thing. So instead, you could make a sweet and spicy dish and have something more exciting and enjoyable.

Your headings should be a different typeface and weight than the body text. So choose two different font families that pair well together for your brand. Then select a font from one family for your headings and a font from the other family for your body text.

Choosing two different fonts for your brand or design is known as font pairing. When pairing typefaces, there are no hard and fast rules. There are no precise formulas. However, some techniques will make the process a lot less daunting.

The goal of pairing fonts is to create a complementary contrast between the styles of text. Avoid pairing fonts that are too similar to each other because it might look like something is wrong or a little off. Likewise, avoid pairing fonts that are two different personalities or different moods.

When selecting the font families for your brand,

look for ones that match or blend in with your brand's personality. For example, if your brand is a bit traditional, choose traditional style fonts. On the other hand, if your brand is more modern or mechanical, look for more modern fonts.

## Brand Font Guidelines

Is your brand easy and delightful to work with? Or is interacting with your brand a chore with challenges at every step? Your choice of the fonts you use in your marketing materials impacts your brand's reputation. Here are some tips for choosing great fonts for your brand.

## Your Fonts Don't Need to Match Your Logo

Looking professional and having an attractive brand takes more than using the same font for your text and logo. Your logo is part of the design of a marketing asset but doesn't count in the two-font guideline. However, you must make sure that the fonts you choose for your headings and body text complement your logo. The three must go well together because they will always be seen together.

## Choose Fonts That Are Easy to Read

Whether it's in print, on a web page, or on an app,

your font choices should create contrast and visual interest. But also make sure the text is easy to read, especially at first glance.

When people first go to a website, they decide whether to stay or bounce away in a fraction of a second. If they choose to stick around, they will scan the page for the information they're looking for, looking at the headings as they scroll from the top down to the bottom.

A font may look pretty, but people won't bother and will move on if it's too hard to read. For example, a signature font may look great for short words or logos. But when used for headings, it takes more time to read and forces the reader to work harder—making it more likely that they'll stop reading.

## Avoid Fonts with Inconsistent Spacing

Avoid fonts where the spacing between the letters doesn't look consistent. The spacing between letters can be adjusted in logos and graphics but will become a burden when used on a text block. The strange spacing will be noticed by prospects when they read the text too.

## Choose Font Families with Multiple Weights and Styles

Only choose font families for your brand with at least Regular, Bold, and Italic fonts. So many times, I have come across a beautiful font family that's perfect for my brand—only to find out that the designer only created one or two weights or styles. When that happens, I have to let that font family go and continue searching for another one.

There will be times when you need the Regular, Bold, and Italic versions. If you don't have them, your computer has to create them artificially. The results can have readability and noticeable problems.

## Headings Font Guidelines

Headings and subheadings help organize and guide readers through your text. Headings are usually the most prominent text sizes in a design, enabling you to choose a font family with more personality and style. Here are some ideas for a great headline font family:

Sans-serif, Serif, Slab Serif, Script, Monospaced, and handwritten fonts can work well as headings. But you must make sure that the font family is easy to read. Use the display version of the typeface if it's available. Use weight, italics, and all capital letters to add or increase contrast.

## Body Text Font Guidelines

Body text is what communicates your message to prospects and turns them into customers. Choose only Serif or Sans-serif font families as body text. Regular, Normal, Book, and Medium, are the best choices of font weights to use as your body text. Avoid using Monospaced fonts because they take more time to read. Finally, make sure the body text is easy to read to avoid it hurting your marketing efforts.

## Call-To-Action Font Guidelines

The job of the call-to-action text is to grab people's attention and encourage them to take action. So, you will use the call-to-action text with buttons and attention-grabbers. But remember, you want to avoid using more than two fonts in your brand. So choose either your headings or body text font family to use in your call-to-action elements. Use Bold, Regular, Normal, Book, or Medium font weights.

## Pick Your Brand's Font Families

It's time to pick two font families for your brand. You will need to choose the fonts for headings, body text, and calls-to-action (i.e., buttons). These font selections will fit most of your needs for creating marketing materials, including websites, marketing funnels, business cards, and more. You can also use your font choices in social media post images and ad images.

Limit your brand to two font family choices to keep your brand looking professional. Your call-to-action font should be either the same font family as your heading or body text. Don't use a new font family for your call-to-action text.

For example, in a web page for your website or marketing funnel, the headings font is applied to your heading tags (i.e., H1 through H6 tags). You will then use the body text font for the body text of the page. Finally, you will apply your call-to-action font to the buttons.

Remember, you can use the same font family for your headings, body text, and call-to-action text. Your brand just won't have much of a unique personality. Of course, you can also change your brand's fonts at any time. But be sure to change the font in all your marketing materials when you do. Consistency is key to an effective brand.

Here are several options for finding the perfect font family pair for your brand:

**Font Pairing Inspiration from Other Brands**

Another simple way to find font families for your brand is to get inspiration from other brands. You can get the font pairing of other brands in your tribe or companies that match your brand's personality. I like to look at retail store brands that my tribe enjoys for design inspiration, especially specialty clothing stores.

CSS Peeper is a plugin for the Chrome browser that makes it easy to discover which font families a website uses. It reveals not only the colors a website is using but also the fonts used. Install the CSS Peeper plugin into your Chrome browser, then visit the website of the inspiration brand. Activate the CSS Peeper plugin by clicking on the extension icon and then clicking on CSS Peeper.

Once activated, CSS Peeper will show you a window over the top of the web page with the colors and fonts used across the entire page. In addition, you can click on any text on the web page to find out which font is used.

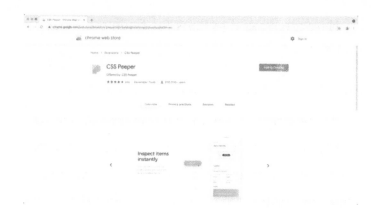

You will likely discover that a website will list several fonts in the font family section separated by commas. The first font family in the list is the one you are looking for. The other fonts are just fallback fonts in case the first font doesn't load properly.

Birchlane.com, for example, is using the Mulireg font family on its site. Sometimes they also use the Quincy font family for the headings. A quick web search for "Mulireg font" reveals that the real font family is Muli, the regular weight, and is available on Adobe Fonts. A search for "Quincy font" shows that Connary Fagen created the font.

The font family is available on several digital marketplaces and at connary.com. This could be a good font pairing for your brand if Birch Lane is a brand that your tribe likes. Quincy and Muli could also be a good pairing if Sincerity is your brand's personality type. Later on, I will show you how to find the Google Font alternatives to these font families.

## Pairing Fonts from Font Superfamilies

One of the easiest ways to pair fonts is to choose two font families from the same font superfamily, such as the Roboto font superfamily. For example, you could select the Roboto Slab for your headings font family and Roboto for your body text.

Here are some different superfamilies that are available on Google fonts:

- PT Serif + PT Sans
- Source Serif Pro + Source Sans Pro
- Alegreya + Alegreya Sans
- Roboto + Roboto Slab
- Merriweather + Merriweather Sans
- Droid Serif + Droid Sans

**Font Pairing Generator**

Fontjoy (fontjoy.com) lets you generate a pairing of fonts from Google Fonts with the amount of contrast and appearance you want, such as high contrast or balanced font combinations. You can paste any copy you intend to use. You can also manually choose fonts to see the best options for pairing. Use this tool to quickly explore font pairings if you only want to use fonts from Google Fonts.

## Pair a Serif with a Sans-Serif Font

One of the easiest ways to pair font families is to choose a Serif font family and a Sans-serif font family. "Serifs" are the small features at the end of the strokes in some fonts.

I like to think of serifs as the little feet that sometimes appear at the bottom of letters like T and F. Serif fonts like Times New Roman and Garamond have the feet. Whereas Sans-Serif fonts like Arial and Tahoma don't have the little feet.

Serif          Sans Serif

**Serif:** Feet

**Sans-serif:** No Feet

Find a serif font that you like for your brand, then choose a Sans-serif font to pair with it. Or do the opposite, find a Sans-serif font to pair with it.

## Font Pairing from Web Searches

Another simple option for pairing font families is to search the web for (font family name) + "font pairing" and see what others recommend. Explore their recommendations and find a font family pairing that matches your brand's personality and your budget. Use this approach when you come across a font family you like for your brand, but you're unsure which font family to pair with it.

For example, suppose you like the Muli font family from Birch Lane but don't like the Quincy font. First, you would search the web for "Muli font pairing" and look at the results. Then find the paired font name in a separate search using (font name) + "font" to see if it's a good fit.

When I searched for "Muli font pairing," I found that Typewolf recommends pairing Muli with Lora, Canela, and Arbutus Slab. I then did a separate search for "Lora font" and found it's a Google Font family with eight different weights and styles. A web search for "Canela font" revealed a paid font with twelve different weights and styles. But a search for "Arbutus Slab" turned up a Google Font family with only one weight and style. So Lora and Canela are good options for brand fonts. However, Arbutus Slab is not a good option because the font family is missing Bold and Italic fonts.

### Pairing From Google and Adobe

Both Google Fonts and Adobe Fonts give recommended font pairings at the bottom of every font family page. For example, view the web page of a font you like on either Google Font (fonts.google.com) or Adobe Font (fonts.adobe.com). Towards the bottom of the page, you will find recommended font pairings and previews.

Google Fonts gives you the added ability to swap fonts in the heading and body text. It also lets you choose the weight and style for each. After you make a change, Google Font will update the preview for you. Unfortunately, Adobe Fonts doesn't have this functionality.

**Search for Font Pairings**

Pairing fonts for a brand is a widespread challenge for businesses and designers. There are a lot of blog posts and websites available with recommended font pairs for you to explore. I recommend searching the web for either "Google font pairings" or "Adobe font pairings" if you're still unsure which fonts to use. To find the latest trends, you can add the year to your search. Such as "google font pairings" + (year) or "adobe font pairings" + (year).

For the latest recommendations for pairing fonts for your brand, visit this web address:

branddesignsecrets.com/resources

## Test Your Fonts with Your Logo

Open your Brand board presentation. Update the headings, body text, and button text in the Brand board with the fonts you're thinking about using for your brand. Examine how everything looks together so far.

You can adjust the size of the logo or text however you prefer. Look for similar characteristics between the logo and the fonts but also look for some visual differences that create contrast.

If you have not yet bought the fonts you are considering for your brand, test with a preview before buying them. Many digital marketplaces, such as Creative Market, will let you type a word or phrase and see a preview of it in that font. Make the font preview as large as you like, then download the preview or take a screenshot. Then add the preview of the font to your Brand board presentation.

Try different fonts if the one you picked isn't looking quite right, either by downloading them or using previews. Then keep searching until you find the fonts you're happy with for your brand.

Remember to save the changes to your Brand board before moving on.

**Pick Google Fonts Alternatives**

Suppose you have chosen a font family that is not from Google Fonts. In that case, I recommend picking a Google Font alternative as well. You'll need it for those times when you're using a web application that only lets you choose Google Fonts. A fast way to find a Google Font alternative is to search the web for (font name) + "font google font alternative," such as "Which google font is closest to Helvetica."

Earlier, we explored the Muli font family that Birch Lane uses and discovered it's a paid font. If you chose this font for your brand, you would need to find a Google Font alternative. A quick web search for "muli font google font alternative" showed that Mulish is a close alternative to the Muli font family. The Mulish font does include the Regular, Bold, and Italic fonts. So Mulish would be a good Google Fonts alternative to Muli.

For an updated list of resources for finding the perfect font pairings for your brand, visit the following web address:

branddesignsecrets.com/resources

## Add Google Fonts Alternatives to Your Brand Board

If you chose Google Fonts alternatives for your brand, open your Brand board presentation. Test your Google Fonts alternative on a second slide. Duplicate the first slide, then change the fonts on the new slide to your Google Fonts alternatives.

Save the changes to your Brand board presentation.

## Download Your Brand and Alternative Fonts

After you have chosen the font families for your brand, download the font files to your computer. If the fonts need to be purchased, buy at least the desktop license. Next, place the font files with your brand logos and other brand-related files. Then install the fonts on your computer to use them when creating presentations and other marketing materials for your business. Finally, make a note for yourself to buy a different license for web fonts, e-publishing, or using an app if you need to.

## Be Consistent With Brand Fonts

Consistency is critical to the success of your brand. Use the same fonts in your online and offline marketing assets. The fonts you use on your website should be the same fonts used in printed brochures and business cards—in every experience customers and prospects have with your company. They should be in alignment to help reinforce your brand and create a memorable impression.

# Step 9
# Brand Colors

———— ❧ ————

The colors you choose for your brand can help you attract customers, create a mood, or make a statement. But selecting the color palette for your brand can seem like a daunting task. There are so many factors to consider:

- What colors will your customers respond to?
- Which colors work well with your products?
- How can you make your brand stand out?

You may have a color or two in mind or your brand's logo. However, you should keep in mind some things when picking colors for your brand to get attention and show off your personality.

When considering brand colors, many business owners think about brands owning a color, such as the Coca-Cola red or the Tiffany & Co. blue. But don't think of "owning" a color as having a copyright. Instead, think about owning the color as you are the only brand (or one of a few) using that color in your market.

By the way, your brand doesn't need to own a single color either. It can use a unique combination of colors in your market to help your brand stand out. Your brand will need a color palette (aka color scheme) whether your brand owns color in your market or not.

For example, Starbucks doesn't use only the green color from its logo in its website, stores, and app. Instead, Starbucks choses several other colors that harmonize with the green logo for its brand, creating its brand's color palette.

You can see the other colors in the Starbuck brand by visiting creative.starbucks.com/color.

**Before Creating Your Brand Color Palette**

Before you start picking the colors for your color palette, there are a couple of things to know and understand.

**Color Models**

You're going to come across a wide variety of different color models when designing and using your brand—color models such as HEX, RGBA, CMYK, and others. Color models are recipes that people and computers use to show a specific color.

For printing, two color models you need to know are CMYK and Pantone. CMYK indicates how much of the four source colors (cyan, magenta, yellow, and black) should be combined to print a specific color. You can think of Pantone colors as the paint samples at a hardware store where each color has its own ID number.

The most common color models for screens, monitors, and devices are HEX, RGB, RGBA, HSB, and HSL. HEX and RGB are the most common color codes you will use on websites and apps. But HSB and HSL are the easiest to understand and adjust by hand.

**Hue:** the color in its purest form.

**Saturation:** the intensity or chroma of a hue.

**Brightness/Lightness:** the lightness or darkness of a color.

Whenever I need a brighter or darker version of a color, here are the steps I use the most:

1. Change the color picker to HSB or HSL.

2. Adjust the brightness and saturation.

3. Change the color picker back to HEX or RGB.

Follow this same process anytime you need to change the brightness or saturation of a color.

You should also know that you cannot print every bright lime green, bright red, and bright blue you see on a screen. Printers will print something close to the color, but it won't be the same. So using these colors in your brand is okay but be aware that the colors will change when printed.

## Color Harmonies

As a designer, I know the struggles of creating a brand palette. And I know how much work is involved to find colors that work well together. You can use the color wheel to find colors that suit your brand and direct attention.

The color wheel, or color circle, is a diagram of colors around a circle that shows the relationships between primary and other colors. The primary colors (red, blue, and yellow) are placed at equal distances on the wheel. Secondary colors (purple, green, and orange) are blends of the primary colors and appear halfway between the primary colors. Tertiary and other blends of colors are added between the primary and secondary colors.

In other words, the color wheel is a helpful guide to finding colors that work well with different colors, also known as color harmonies.

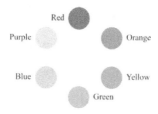

See the color harmony diagrams in color by visiting this web address:

branddesignsecrets.com/resources

## Monochromatic Colors

Monochromatic colors use different shades and tints of the same color as if you were mixing different amounts of black and white with a single color. Monochromatic colors are lighter or darker than each other.

## Complementary Colors

Complementary colors are opposite each other on the color wheel, for instance, red and green. They create a vibrant look when used at full saturation, but they can be jarring. So it's best to only use them sparingly for an accent or pop.

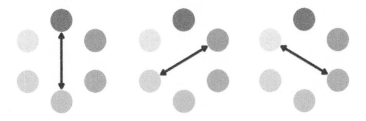

## Split Complementary Colors

Split complementary colors start with one color

and use the two colors next to the opposite (aka complementary) color. This color scheme is similar to the complementary color scheme but has less tension. Split complementary colors are more versatile and less aggressive, making them a good choice for brands that want something energetic but subtle.

## Analogous Colors

Analogous colors are next to each other on the color wheel. They create a comforting and balanced look that is often found in nature. Analogous colors are harmonious and pleasing to the eye.

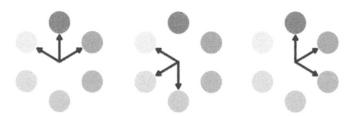

## Triadic Colors

Triadic colors are three colors evenly spaced around the color wheel, such as red, yellow, and green. They tend to be vibrant but not as jarring as complementary color schemes can be. Using tints and shades of triadic colors can bring calmness, while full brightness can be highly energetic and youthful.

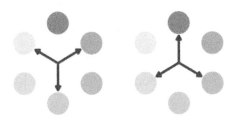

**Tetradic (aka Square) Colors**

Tetradic colors are two sets of complementary colors that create a set of four colors. Square colors are the same but evenly spaced around the color wheel. Striking the right balance with these colors can be challenging because there are four colors involved. But these rich color schemes give plenty of variation and can be very eye-catching.

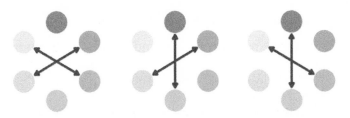

I use Adobe Color (color.adobe.com) to explore the color harmonies related to a logo and create a brand color scheme. But it's not the only color tool

I use. Later on, I'll show you the two color tools I use the most for creating brand color palettes.

## Use Pure Black and White with Caution

The combination of pure black and white is overpowering and unsettling, so use it with caution. Black text on a white background becomes too much for the eyes to read, especially if there's a lot of text, for example, on a web page or in an app.

The same goes for white text on a black background. White letters will visually bleed onto the black background, especially when people look at the screen for too long. The contrast will create a halo or halation effect.

Use a very dark shade of color instead of pure black. The result will look less unsettling and more natural because black is an artificial color. In nature, dark and light objects absorb the color around them. Shadows are not pure black, and clouds are not pure white.

When choosing the colors for your brand, avoid choosing pure white, pure black, or neutral grey. That is unless pure black and white is part of the aesthetic of your brand. You can use white, black, and neutral gray in nearly any design because they coordinate with any colors. Therefore it's usually not necessary to specify them as part of your brand. But, as you'll see, you will include at least one neutral shade in your palette to help balance your brand.

**Creating Brand Color Palettes**

Choosing colors that work well together and define your brand colors is an art. It's not a science. It should be based on what looks good, not what the numbers say. I will show you the color generators that I use the most. But consider the colors they generate as a starting point. Don't be afraid to slightly change any colors to suit your needs and your brand.

But consistency is a critical factor in branding. So don't adjust the hue of your brand colors after you have chosen them. You can change the lightness and darkness and even combine the colors, but the hues should always stay the same.

**Coolors**

Coolors (coolors.co) is a simple color palette generator popular with designers and non-designers. The color combinations that it creates are unique and look great. After starting the generator, you only need to press your space bar to see a beautiful new color palette.

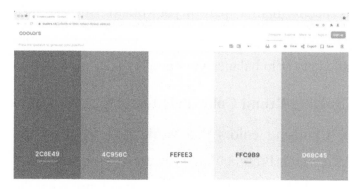

The code at the bottom of each color is the HEX value of that color. This is very convenient for using on a website but challenging to understand. Click on the HEX number to copy the code but also to change the color model. Change to HSB or HSL to adjust the color, then change it back to HEX before creating more colors.

Place your mouse over one of the colors, and several options appear. Next, click the lock icon to "lock" that color in place. Coolors will then use the locked color as inspiration and pick other colors to go with it. You can even lock more than one color, which is something I do pretty often.

It's also common for me to find colors that I like, but I'm unsure about. So I press the space bar and continue looking. That's when I realize that the previous color scheme was worth saving. Fortunately, a back arrow in the top navigation lets you revisit the color palettes you previously looked at. Each time you click the back button, you go back to a color palette.

I don't like to leave my brand colors up to chance and prefer to set the direction Coolors takes me. I typically use Coolors after I already have a starting color. So start with a color picked using the CSS Peeper Chrome plugin or colors from your logo. Click on the HEX code at the bottom of the color, and you can paste the HEX code of another color. That's how Coolors lets you specify a color and create a color palette from it. Just be sure to lock that color before you generate the other colors.

When you have a color palette that you like, you will probably want to save it. In the top menu, click the Export button to save the color palette to your computer. I usually export the colors as an image, but the PDF is useful too.

## Colormind

Colormind's Website Colors generator (colormind.io/bootstrap) is another color palette generator I like to use. Click the Generate button, and Colormind will create a new color palette.

However, Colormind's Website Colors will create a color palette with specific uses on a website. So Colormind is a color generator to use with Coolors. After you generate a new color palette with Colormind's Website Colors, scroll down to see how the colors might look on a website.

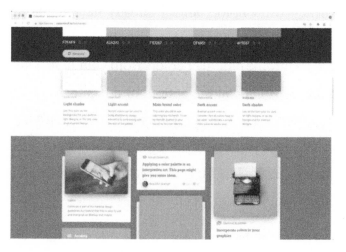

You can specify a color before generating a palette by clicking the sliders icon below a color. You can also lock a color before generating a palette using the lock icon. Unfortunately, Colormind does not have a back button or an export option. That means you won't be able to go back to a previously generated color palette or save it.

Here's how I use Colormind's Website Colors generator:

1. Create a color palette using Coolors, then pick one of the five colors as the main color, like a color from your logo.
2. Visit the Colormind's Website Colors generator website (colormind.io/bootstrap).
3. Enter the main color from Coolors as the middle color in Colormind's Website Colors generator.
4. Lock the color in.
5. Click the Generate button.

This process gives me a color palette with nine colors that harmonize well together.

## Colors from a Photo

If you lack inspiration and don't want to spend a lot of time searching for the right colors, photos can be a great place to start. In fact, photos are one of the best ways to find natural color palettes for your brand. First, find a photo with colors you like for a brand, then use a generator to create a color palette.

My favorite tool for creating color palettes from a photo is iColorpalette (icolorpalette.com/color-palette-from-images). iColorpalette is my tool of choice because it shows you more than just the four or five most used colors, helping you find the small accent colors that might appear in the photo.

You can upload a photo to iColorpalette or enter the web address (aka URL) of an image from the web. After the picture has been uploaded, iColorpalette will show you the five most used colors in the photo, along with a preview of the image. Scroll down the page to see more colors from the picture. From there, you can download a PDF file containing all the colors generated from the photo.

Sometimes all the colors I need I can find from iColorpalette, but other times I need more. When I need more or different colors, I use Coolors and Colormind to help create them.

Don't be afraid to use more than one tool to help create the perfect colors for your brand.

## Colors from a Brand's Website

Earlier I mentioned that other websites could be a great source of color inspiration, especially retail, e-commerce, and boutique websites. These specialty retail websites must target a particular group of people to attract customers in an "Everything's on Amazon" business environment. Using the colors they have chosen as a starting point lets you leverage the research they've already done.

Often, the colors of the products they are selling are used as the colors in their logo. Instead of using CSS Peeper, take a screenshot of the website then upload it to iColorpalette for color inspiration. Then use Coolors and Colormind to expand your brand's color palette.

## Create Your Brand's Color Palette

Use any of these tools or processes to create the color palette for your brand. Choose at least five colors, then pick one of the five as your main color.

I typically end up with nine colors because I use Coolors and Colormind together.

If your logos don't have colors yet or you're open to changing them, follow these steps to create your brand's color palette:

1. Take a screenshot of a brand's website that your tribe likes.
2. Upload the screenshot to iColorpalette (icolorpalette.com/color-palette-from-images).
3. Download the colors from iColorpalette as a PDF file.
4. Choose up to five colors from the PDF file for your brand.
5. Use Coolors (coolors.co) to fill in the missing colors if you have less than five colors.
6. Download the colors as a PDF file from Coolors if you used it.
7. Pick your main brand color from the five colors.
8. Copy the HEX code for your main color.
9. Visit Colormind's Website Colors generator (colormind.io/bootstrap).

10. Below the middle color, click the sliders icon (next to the lock icon) and paste the HEX code for your main color.

11. Lock the middle color.

12. Click the Generate button.

13. Take a screenshot of the Colormind colors, including a screenshot of the webpage sample section.

If your logos already have colors and you want to keep them, follow these steps to create your brand's color palette:

1. Visit Coolors (coolors.co) and enter in the colors of your logo.

2. Lock each of the colors before generating other colors.

3. Press the space bar to generate colors that harmonize with the colors from your logo.

4. Lock the colors you like before generating new ones.

5. Stop when you have five colors that you want for your brand.

6. Export the five colors for your brand as a PDF file.

7. If your logo has more than one color, pick one color as the main color for your brand.

8. Copy the HEX code for the main color of your logo.

9. Visit Colormind's Website Colors generator (colormind.io/bootstrap.)

10. Below the middle color, click the sliders icon (next to the lock icon) and paste the HEX code for your main color.

11. Lock the middle color.

12. Click the Generate button.

13. Take screenshots of the Colormind colors, including a screenshot of the webpage sample section.

At the end of this process, you will have at least nine colors to use in your brand. Nine colors give you many options that will come in handy when you start designing your marketing assets.

For the latest recommendations for finding great colors for your brand, visit the following web address:

branddesignsecrets.com/resources

### Test Your Brand Colors

Open the Brand board you've been working on so far. Change the colors of the Brand presentation to the colors of your brand. Try changing the colors of your heading, body text, and even the background color.

Play with the presentation. Get a sense of how well the colors coordinate with the rest of the board. You might even create multiple slides with different colors.

Adjust the brightness and saturation of your brand colors when using them. You can make them lighter or darker, more saturated or less saturated. Play with the colors to find color combinations that go together and match the energy of your brand.

Is the text visually attractive and professional-looking?

Which words would you use to describe the style of your new brand?

Does the combination match the personality of the brand you originally envisioned?

You can choose a different font if the ones you initially chose don't look as good as you thought they would. If something doesn't look right with the colors, you can change the colors. Either adjust the hue or use Coolors to find another color. After you find a better color, update your Brand board with the new colors.

Use this presentation as your chance to play with and refine your brand. Now is the time to make adjustments and corrections to your brand before creating new marketing assets.

# Case Study
# Untapped Customers

———— ❧ ————

## The Challenge

During the COVID-19 pandemic of 2020, I watched friends and acquaintances struggle with their current business. Some were having to figure out how to pivot their business to an online-only model to survive. Others were launching new business ventures with the spare time they were suddenly given.

By talking to many of them, I found designing for themselves and hiring designers were real struggles. So I started helping them create new marketing assets and strategies for investing in design in stages. Eventually, I decided to rename my company to Untapped Customers and focus on helping small business owners—starting with helping business owners design and build their brand elements.

From my startup experience, I know that

establishing a company's brand saves time and creates a consistent look and feel.

All the digital marketing services have templates. Canva is filled with them, and so are the various funnel builders, email marketing providers, and website builders. But none of those templates match each other and don't match the unique personality of your company.

Defining your brand's visuals ends the guessing and lets you quickly update the designs of each asset to match your brand—reassuring people that they're in the right place at every step along the journey to becoming a customer. Defining your brand's images makes your company stand out and become more memorable.

Changing the focus of my business and renaming it created the new challenge of updating my company's brand. A challenge to attract a new audience with a brand that stands out and captivates my perfect customers. A challenge to go from a clean slate to a complete brand as quickly as possible. Then using that brand to design my lead magnets, funnels, slide decks, website, and more.

## The Implementation

I started building the strategy for Untapped Customers by learning about the market and looking for opportunities to stand out. Small business owners earning less than $10,000 per month became my primary target audience. Those earning more than $10,000 per month were my secondary target audience. This distinction was necessary because a business is at very different stages before and after the $10,000 per month milestone.

My customer avatars included a real estate agent, a chiropractor, a personal trainer, and a hypnotherapist. With my customer avatars created, I put my attention towards the competition. First, I looked at the websites and funnels being utilized by my direct competitors. I then created a Direct Competition board, as detailed in the "Your Competition" chapter. Right away, I started noticing a pattern of corporate styling. Many were very serious looking and made heavy use of blue, gold, and black tones. They looked like corporations trying to attract people who work at other corporations. Nearly all of them were aiming for a Competency personality type. The others opted for more of a Sincerity personality type.

While the competition took the 9–5 corporate route, Untapped Customer's tribe enjoyed the weekend instead. They were bucking the 40-hour workweek trend and enjoying life. They were expressive and creative. Most of the websites used white backgrounds with fun and cheerful colors. They love helping other people achieve their dreams and taking the road less traveled.

The disconnect between the competition styling and Untapped Customers' tribe meant an opportunity to stand out and be magnetic. Instead of adopting a safe corporate styling, Untapped Customers should be more sincere, approachable, and fun. It should use lighter and white backgrounds and cheerful colors.

After understanding where the Untapped Customers' brand can fit in the market, I could design the brand. I was drawn to the iceberg symbol for the brand mark and logos. It summarizes my belief that there are so many opportunities for a business than their owners might see right now, such as opportunities to help more customers and more ways to grow.

Showing the bottom of the iceberg was essential to me because it represents their potential business.

The bottom also needed to be large to reinforce the notion that its potential is more extensive than where it is now. Without showing the bottom, people might think it was smaller or the same

But an iceberg is a challenging visual to simplify. Without adding water to the symbol, the iceberg looks like an odd-shaped diamond or triangle. When an iceberg icon is small, such as in a webpage's favicon, it's also tricky to recognize as an iceberg.

These challenges didn't mean the iceberg metaphor was impossible, though. It only meant that I would need to spend a lot of time exploring ideas and trying different approaches before arriving at the perfect logo.

**The Outcome**

At first, I started exploring the hand-drawn boutique vibe for the brand. I was also trying to stay within a Sincerity personality type. That didn't work, so I began exploring a more scripted calligraphy style of logo. Some felt too vintage, yet others felt expressive, active, and adventurous.

But what was the type of energy I wanted for the

Untapped Customers brand? Not knowing which direction to go was causing me to wander aimlessly. How do I want my customers to feel when interacting with my brand? What are some of the emotions they will go through while working with the company? After some exploration of phrases and photographs, I finally landed on two words: road trip. It was a perfect fit.

Building a business is an adventure, but you get to choose how extreme you take it. You can blaze your own trail if you wish. But my perfect customers are looking for the right path to take them where they want to go. It doesn't matter if the roads are paved or not, as long as they have guidance along the way. The journey to get to their goal is part of the adventure, and it's even more fun when they have friends along for the ride.

I knew I needed to avoid the Ruggedness personality type but could opt for the Excitement personality type. My customer avatars enjoy going outside and having an adventure. But being dropped in the middle of a forest and "living off the land" isn't their idea of fun.

I started adding road trip photos to my logo

Inspiration board. Then I began looking for textures and patterns for the brand. Textures of asphalt, concrete, maps, and cars spoke to the road trip theme but were too literal. The Pinterest board felt more appropriate for car, car insurance, and road assistance companies than Untapped Customers.

While looking through background patterns on Creative Market, I came across images of warped backgrounds. The high contrast between the black and white lines seemed too aggressive, but I liked the movement the pattern created. The design also harmonized well with some illustrations I wanted to use. The combination of the pattern and illustrations set the tone for the brand's visual identity: clean organic. This meant it could use hand-drawn or cut-out shapes without a rough pencil texture.

The wordmark logo came together quickly after finding a script font I liked. But the struggle of using the iceberg image continued until I added a flag to the mix. At that moment, the symbol shifted from "potential" to "accomplishment" and "territory." The flag also allowed the brand to have a more comprehensive selection of logos to fit nearly any size.

At full size, the brand mark shows the entire iceberg and flag combined. But the combination is very tall and won't work well when the logo needs to be short. A second logo was created using only the top of the iceberg and the flag. It told a story of success and accomplishment, which my customer avatars want to achieve.

When an even smaller logo is needed, just the flag can be used and recognized. This responsive logo approach gives the Untapped Customers brand a lot of versatility. It allows the brand to be consistent and recognizable in nearly all sizes.

When designing your brand, you don't need to have a lot of variations of your logo. But you'll have to represent your brand in small sizes on occasions because even the avatars for your social media accounts are tiny sometimes.

I added the logos to a new Brand board to assist with picking the typography and colors. Being able to see everything in one place really helps. I also added example photography and patterns for a complete representation of the brand so far.

I didn't want the brand to move too far away from what the tribe already likes. My goal is always to strike a balance between similarities and differences. The chosen patterns and illustrations were different enough that I could use similar fonts to other tribe brands. So I looked at the font pairings other brands were using. One was using Minion and Brandon Grotesque, and I like the style and contrast. But they felt a little too safe and didn't coordinate very well with the logo.

I searched for "Fonts similar to Minion" and "Fonts similar to Brandon Grotesque" on the web. Eventually, I found the New Spirit font family on Adobe Fonts. New Spirit has a lot of personality with some retro flair. I already had a subscription to Adobe Creative Cloud, so I activated New Spirit on my computer. Then I added it to the Brand board to see how well it worked with the font. The angles of the font go well with the script font used in the logo.

I picked Acumin Pro for the body text because it's simple and doesn't demand too much attention. Using Acumin directs all the attention to the headings. Both New Spirit and Acumin font families also have a variety of thicknesses and styles, giving the Untapped Customers brand more flexibility.

Adobe Fonts (New Spirit, Acumin Pro)

**Attract Your Perfect Audience, Create Faster, Grow Your Business**

People need your help and they're ready to pay you for it. Stop the frustration, guessing, and invisibility. Start attracting the perfect audience to grow your business.

Google Fonts (Source Serif Pro, Source Sans Pro)

**Attract Your Perfect Audience, Create Faster, Grow Your Business**

People need your help and they're ready to pay you for it. Stop the frustration, guessing, and invisibility. Start attracting the perfect audience to grow your business.

Since the brand is using Adobe fonts, I needed to choose some Google Fonts alternatives. I searched for "New spirit google font alternative," but the results didn't turn up options I liked. So I put the New Spirit font aside and decided to focus on Acumin. I searched for "Acumin google font alternative," and Source Sans Pro came up.

Sans in the font name told me this font might be part of a font family. A quick search on Google Fonts for "source" revealed there was a Source Serif Pro too. Even better, Source Serif Pro had many of the characteristics of New Spirit and several fonts in the family. Thus making Source Serif Pro and Source Sans Pro the Google Font alternatives for the Untapped Customers brand.

I started the Untapped Customers color palette by drawing inspiration from my Tribe Pinterest board. Colors similar to the Canva logo appeared on a few other sites, along with mint green, some soft reds, and vibrant orange. I used iColorpalette to get the colors from website screenshots. I then used Coolors to explore combinations of the colors. Basically, what would happen if I used these two colors to start in Coolors?

The colors from the Tribe board were too soft and comfortable—not quite matching the adventurous and joyful energy I was looking for. But Coolors started showing me colors that better fit the brand. As I found a color I liked, I locked it inside Coolors to create other colors. I exported the palette as an image and added the color to the Brand board. Then with many color options available, I could start narrowing down the other colors.

The Untapped Customers brand needed two colors, one for the wordmark and another for the brand mark. The brand also needed at least three secondary colors before moving on. The final step was to use Colormind to create more neutral tones and complete the color palette.

The result is a brand identity for Untapped Customers that stands out and speaks to its target audience. When using any funnel or website builder for Untapped Customers, I already know which fonts, colors, and backgrounds to use. In addition, the brand board contains references to the photography and illustrations that match the brand—simplifying the decision-making process and saving time. Untapped Customers is now on its way to helping small business owners on their journey to growing their business and enjoying the ride along the way.

See the completed brand board for Untapped Customers by visiting the following web address:

branddesignsecrets.com/resources

# Step 10
# Refining Your Brand

——— ❖ ———

There you have it, the entire Magnetic Brand formula. Everything you need to design a brand for your business that stands out in the market and helps it grow. You've learned every step in the process. You saw how I used the steps to design one of my own brands. You even built a brand board for your new brand along the way.

It's time to date your brand before you marry it!

Get feedback on your Brand board from five to eight of your customers or people that fit in your tribe. You need to show it to at least five people to balance out one person's personal preferences. Limit feedback to a maximum of eight people to optimize your time and not get overwhelmed.

When asking for feedback, don't let them know you designed it. People generally want to make other people feel good. They will naturally hold back honest criticism if they know you created the brand.

Instead, tell them someone else designed the brand and you would like their honest perspective.

Also, let them know the design is a work in progress. You created a beautiful brand, and people will inherently see that you put a lot of work into it. They will avoid giving you all their feedback because they don't want to cause more work for you. By letting them know it's a work in progress, you're permitting them to give you all of their feedback.

Write down notes of everyone's feedback on pieces of paper for yourself. After showing the Brand board to everyone, go through your notes. Look for patterns in the feedback instead of focusing on those from one person. For example, one person saying they don't like a color is far different from five people saying they don't like a color.

Make adjustments to your brand based on the feedback, especially the issues mentioned by several people. Of course, it's okay to say "no" to some feedback too. You don't have to make every change that one person recommended. But give more credit to issues multiple people identified.

After making changes based on the feedback, you can either gather more feedback or start using your brand. Aim for striking a balance between getting feedback and launching your brand. Don't wait until your brand is perfect to launch it. You can update your brand at any time, and it won't help your business until you start using it.

You gained clarity about your market and the people you want to help. You designed a brand identity that represents your company and its unique personality so that it can shine. You've validated your design by getting feedback giving you more confidence in your choices.

It's time to start putting your new brand out there for the world to see. Start attracting more of your perfect customers. Start looking like the type of business that they want to work with. Because once it's out there, your business is going to get more attention, more customers, and more five-star reviews.

# Step 11
# Launch Your Brand

———— ❧ ————

Y ou're ready to launch your brand and get your company the exposure it deserves. So, where do you go from here? What do you do next? The answer is simple: start selling with your new brand.

Make a list of the places where your prospects and customers interact with your brand. Then start updating those parts with your new brand. For example, use your brand to create new business cards for yourself and your team. Update your social media avatars and profile images with your brand. You might even need to update your invoices and email footers with your new brand.

Use your new brand on your website and marketing funnel web pages. Use your Brand board as inspiration for the changes to make. Put your new logo at the top and in the footer. Update the fonts and colors to match your Brand board. If you are running a webinar, you can even update your webinar slide deck to show off your new brand.

If you're feeling overwhelmed, several resources and options are available to you on the resources page for this book. I tell you how to connect with others and get feedback on your brand or the next steps. You can see other brands that have been designed using the Magnetic Brand Method. You can even see how you can work directly with my team and me.

See all the book resources available to you by visiting the following web address:

branddesignsecrets.com/resources

**Congratulations!**

You've done the work, and the future is ready for you. You're getting started and doing great. You have the courage and the confidence to put your brand out there, and you know it looks professional. Feel good and confident in the brand you created.

I'm so happy for you. I'm excited to see where your company and brand go from here!

Made in the USA
Las Vegas, NV
25 April 2022

47978716R00114